FUNDRAISING
FOR A
COMMUNITY
PROJECT

FUNDRAISING
FOR A
COMMUNITY
PROJECT

How to research grants and secure financing
for local groups and projects in the UK

SIMON WHALEY

howtobooks

Published by How To Books Ltd,
Spring Hill House, Spring Hill Road,
Begbroke, Oxford OX5 1RX, United Kingdom.
Tel: (01865) 375794. Fax: (01865) 379162.
info@howtobooks.co.uk
www.howtobooks.co.uk

British Library Cataloguing in Publication Data
A catalogue record for this book is available from the British Library

ISBN 978 1 84528 174 8

Cover design by Baseline Arts Ltd, Oxford
Produced for How To Books by Deer Park Productions, Tavistock, Devon
Typeset by PDQ Typesetting, Newcastle-under-Lyme, Staffs.
Printed and bound by Cromwell Press Ltd, Trowbridge, Wiltshire

NOTE: The material contained in this book is set out in good faith for general guidance
and no liability can be accepted for loss or expense incurred as a result of relying in
particular circumstances on statements made in the book. The laws and regulations are
complex and liable to change, and readers should check the current position with the
relevant authorities before making personal arrangements.

Contents

List of Illustrations

Figures

Tables

Preface

In the same way that applying for a grant should be a team effort, writing this book gave me the opportunity to meet up with good friends and work colleagues at Herefordshire Council and the Herefordshire Partnership. I'd therefore like to take this opportunity to thank Penny Jones and her team, including Sara Burch, Tracy Ricketts, Dawn Turner and Clare Wichbold MBE for giving up their time and meeting me. I'd also like to thank Annie Brookes and Helen Jarvis for taking the time to read the first draft of this book and providing me with some useful feedback.

Both the community group and funding organisation that I have used in this book as practical examples are fictitious. The layout and design of the example application forms, offer letters, monitoring and claim forms are also my own creation. With so many real funding organisations out there, there are just as many different designs and formats of those forms. However, the important point is that the information contained within them is an example of the information you will be expected to provide for a real grant application and claim.

It's always nice to know how useful readers have found a book, so if you have any comments, I'd be delighted to see them; you can email them to communityprojectfunding@simonwhaley.co.uk. I wish you every success with your project.

Simon Whaley

Introduction

No one has an automatic right to a grant. Ouch, that probably hurt, but it needs to be said. If you want someone to give you some money, then you have to jump however high they ask you to jump. You might think that they are being bureaucratic or obstructive but funders can reasonably ask you to do whatever they like – it is, after all, *their* money that *you* will be spending. However, funders are not mean-spirited organisations! They are keen for community groups to apply for funding and improve their local communities. So, whilst you may be asked to jump through several hoops for a grant, a good funder will help train you to get through those hoops. Successful grant applications are based upon a good funder–applicant relationship.

Many people don't like the hassle of having to produce what might be perceived as plenty of paperwork, and as a result they dismiss this vital source of money. Getting their project off the ground then becomes more difficult.

Jumble and car boot sales are a favoured fundraising method used by community groups up and down the country. They can raise a few hundred pounds or several thousand, but ultimately they have their limits. There has to be another way to fund your community project – and there is. You can apply for a grant. A grant will solve your problem – won't it?

Grant funding can solve your financial predicament, but it may also provide you with new challenges. It can, however, turn your project from one that doesn't get off the ground to one that gets finished and, more importantly, used.

WHAT IS A GRANT?

A grant is not a loan. That means you don't have to pay back the money if you complete your project in the way you said you would on your grant application form. But neither is it a handout for you to go and spend as you please.

> A GRANT IS AN AMOUNT OF MONEY, GIVEN BY AN
> ORGANISATION FOR A SPECIFIC PURPOSE

There are thousands of grant-making bodies in the United Kingdom, all eager to help communities and community groups like yours, to better themselves. You might be looking for a few hundred pounds to brighten up a bare patch of ground on the village green or a few thousand pounds to print an information leaflet to help attract tourists to your area. Perhaps you're looking for several tens of thousands of pounds to help put an extension on your community centre. Whatever you are looking to achieve, the chances are that there is an organisation out there willing to help in some way. Some groups will find it easier to get support than others. This is because funding organisations have their own priorities about the type of problems they'd like their money to help solve. The challenge is often finding the right organisation or enough organisations to enable you to fund your entire project.

Once you've found an organisation (or several) who you think might be willing to support you, it is then necessary to start looking at what you have to do to get hold of that money. There will be times when you wonder whether all of this effort is worth it. It is. Remember what you will be able to achieve once you've been awarded the money.

Yes, you will have to jump through hoops to satisfy your funder's requirements and you might have to jump quite high in order to do it. It may seem infuriating when a funder asks you to carry out a survey of your community to prove that there is a demand for your project when you already know there is. Whilst it may be frustrating, there is a reason for them doing this, and that's what this book will help you to understand. The funders are also there to help you, so use them and their expertise to your advantage. It is in their interest to award grants to projects that will have an impact.

With so many funding bodies out there, it is impossible to cover them all in this book. The aim is to give you a basic understanding of the grant application process, which should improve the quality of your application, and therefore your chances of success. For many grants, you will have to provide a lot of information to enable the funding organisation to assess your application. Applying to the wrong organisation is therefore a waste of your time and your funder's. It can also be very demoralising.

Still determined to make a difference in your community? Good. Then read on to discover how to make applying for funding easier. Try to read all ten chapters before making a start on your application. Understanding how the whole grant process works from beginning to end will reduce frustration in the future. It will help to put everything into context. Forewarned is forearmed as they say, but please don't view this as a battle! Applying for funding is all about forging good relationships, not getting one over on the enemy!

1
You and Your Project

Before you can begin applying for any grant money, you need to make sure that your own house is in order first. Act professionally and funders will treat you with respect.

WHO ARE YOU?

Funders who award money to community projects will offer the money to the organisation running the project and not an individual. You therefore need to ensure that your group is a properly constituted group before you begin completing an application form. This sounds much grander than it is in practice, and the chances are, your group is already constituted even though you may not realise it!

A constitution is a set of rules that details how your group is run. It should state:

- the activities your group undertakes;
- where this takes place;
- who runs the group.

It may also include information about how new members can join, what the membership fees are and any disciplinary procedures you may have should anyone in the group bring it into disrepute.

The important point to remember with your funding application is that although you may put your name and address on the form as the group contact, it is your organisation applying for the grant, not you as an individual. If your application is successful, then the funding organisation will offer the grant money to the group, not to you, even though they may address their letter to you at home. If you have to sign any paperwork, then you are signing on behalf of the group. You should make this clear by stating the position you hold in the group. The group's constitution (or some minutes from a committee meeting) should therefore clearly demonstrate to your funders that you have the authority to do this on their behalf. Some funders may also ask to see documentation proving that your project has support from the whole group, and that they are aware of what is going on.

WHAT TYPE OF ORGANISATION ARE YOU?

This book is aimed at community groups, which covers a broad arena. You could be a:

- local sports club;
- community centre management committee;
- school parent–teachers association;
- Women's Institute;
- amateur dramatics group;
- writers' circle;
- reading group;
- faith group;
- history group;
- gardening club;
- parish council;
- photographic group.

In fact, the list is almost endless. A community group is a collection of like-minded individuals with a common interest. Some funders define a community group as one that is a 'not-for-profit' organisation. This means that your group is not set up with the intention of making money to be distributed between the members at the end of the year.

This doesn't mean to say that your group isn't allowed to have savings. The distinction here is that, with a not-for-profit or community group, any savings will be used to benefit the group as a whole, rather than as individuals.

Some community groups establish themselves as trusts or charitable organisations. This gives them more legal rights, but more responsibilities. Look at the funder's guidelines and eligibility criteria if your group is registered as a charity or trust to see if you are still allowed to apply for a grant.

CONSTITUTIONS

A constitution is basically the set of rules for your group. No matter how small a community group is, it should have rules that clearly state how the group is run, its aims and how it intends to achieve them. Many small groups can manage without them, but a constitution ensures that the group is run for the benefit of all its members and should prevent one person from dominating and taking over. Community groups should be democratic! Each group should have someone in charge, such as a Chairperson, and then a Secretary to deal with any correspondence and act as a point of contact, as well as a Treasurer to keep track of money.

As soon as your group starts handling money, then a constitution is a must. With money comes responsibility. This can happen early on if you have to charge a membership fee to cover room hire costs. As soon as you start collecting money you will need to open a bank account in the name of your group. A bank will ask to see a copy of the group's constitution before they'll open an account for you. As well as detailing how your group is run and how often roles such as Chair, Secretary and Treasurer are elected, it should also clarify who should be authorised signatories on the group's bank account. You can have as many roles on your group's committee as you see fit, but too many may make running your group cumbersome.

A constitution demonstrates to all group members (old and new) and outside organisations that your group has a proper structure to ensure that it operates effectively, and that there is a clear decision-making process. A constitution should contain:

- the group's name or title;

- the aims of the group (why you exist);

- how the group will achieve this (what your activities are);

- the local area that your group covers;

- how your group is run (the roles on the committee, where you meet, how often, how decisions are made, etc.);

- what to do if your group stops meeting (what happens to any money you have in the bank, and any assets that the group owns).

Figure 1, at the end of this chapter, is an example constitution for Bevel Gate Gardening Club. Yours may look similar, or it may be completely different. There is no standard format for constitutions. However, it should contain all the information necessary to allow your group to run smoothly and deal with any problems that arise. A constitution is not a fixed document. Review it regularly to ensure that it still meets the needs of your group. If it needs changing, then simply amend it with the agreement of the whole group and arrange for the committee to sign the new version.

YOU NEED A PROFESSIONAL ATTITUDE

If you are looking for someone to give you some money to get your project off the ground then you have to be able to sell it well. That doesn't mean taking a cavalier attitude and trying to tempt an unsuspecting funder to buy into your project as if you were Del or Rodney Trotter from *Only Fools and Horses*. Don't even think about being such a plonker!

Funders expect professionalism. Let's face it, they could be giving you their money, so you really need them. Not only that, but you are also competing for their money. They don't have a limitless supply, and the vast majority of funders receive requests for money far exceeding the amount available. Why should the funder give money to your project instead of someone else's?

If you were a business going to a bank and looking to borrow some money, you would expect to have to produce a raft of facts and figures demonstrating that your idea is sound and there is a minimum amount of risk. If successful, the bank will lend you the money and, of course, because it is a loan, you will be expected to pay it back. A grant-making organisation won't ask for their money back if you actually spend it on what you said you would spend it on. However, they will expect something in return – information and evidence of what your project has achieved.

Charity requests

Do you receive letters from charities asking for donations? In the same way that you are looking for money towards your project, these charity letters are approaching you as a possible 'funder' who might make a donation. Next time you receive one, take a closer look at the information they are giving you. How many times do you see environmental charities say that whilst any amount is gratefully received,

- a £10 donation will help to plant three trees;
- £25 will plant 10 metres of hedgerow;
- or £50 will provide 25 metres of fencing to protect the young plants from predatory animals?

Charities know that they too need to act professionally when asking for money from the general public. How good do you feel knowing that your £10 donation is planting three trees? Unlike a general donation into a charity box, you know exactly what your money is being spent on. The charity has researched its costs and requirements and can clearly demonstrate where your money will be spent. And that's what your potential funders need to know.

Be specific

When funding organisations look at an application form, they want to know what their money is going to be used for, and what impact this will have on the local community. The impact can be direct or indirect, but you need to state clearly what that impact will be. Applying for a grant isn't simply a question of filling out an application form and hoping for the best. It is necessary to supply background information to support your application and any figures you have quoted will need an explanation as to how you arrived at them. To give you an example, if your project needs £500 to hire a piece of equipment, how do you know you need £500? Did you just think of this number? If so, you need to think again – not of another number, but of a way to find out exactly how much you need. For many costs this means obtaining quotes. If you need some work doing on your own house, you'll probably try to get three quotes. Having three quotes gives you a better idea of what the real cost is likely to be.

The same principle applies to obtaining costs for your community project. If you can provide copies of the quotes you have received, the funder will know that you have taken the time and effort to ensure your application is as accurate as possible. If you've taken this much trouble to get the information on your application form correct, it provides an indication as to how thorough you will be when you come to implement your project. Funders are keen to offer grants to projects that will be completed and succeed. If a project fails, then that grant money has been wasted. Not only has the funder lost the money, but so too has another applicant whose project may have succeeded where yours failed.

WHO IS IN CHARGE?

When a community group wants to undertake a project, it should be the group's desire, not the whim of a dominant member of the committee. The constitution should clarify what the decision-making process of the group is, and have safeguards in place to prevent dominant members from taking over and imposing their ideas upon the rest of the group.

Likewise, running a project and applying for the funding should be a group effort. Don't even think about dumping this work on one unsuspecting soul. Putting an application together needs to be a coordinated group effort. Not only will this demonstrate to funders that the project has the support of the group as a whole, but it also gives the whole group ownership of the project.

An application form will often start by asking for a contact name and address for the community group. This person will then become the first point of contact, but that doesn't mean that they have to organise and implement the whole project! They will be the person to whom correspondence and other communications will be sent.

Project working group

A good way to organise yourselves is to create a project working group. This could be a sub-committee of your normal committee and comprise your usual committee members or even group members who are not part of the committee. It's not necessary to make this a very formal group, but the allocation of specific responsibilities for the project will make it clear to everyone in the group (and potential funders) who does what. Naturally, the Treasurer will need to be involved with anything to do with the group's finances and the payment of invoices. They may also get involved with collating all the financial information required for the grant claim forms. Decide who will be the name and address contact for applications, and who will gather supporting information to demonstrate the need for your project. This supporting information may be a job for one person, or the whole group. Does anyone in your group have any experience that you can draw upon? If you're planning an extension to your community centre and a member of your community centre committee happens to be an architect, then they will have an understanding of the planning application process. Some funders like to appraise project applications using a panel process, which may involve giving you the opportunity to make a presentation to them (see Chapter 6). Make the most of your group's existing skills and get someone involved who is used to doing presentations in their day job. That way, when the time comes, that person will know the project inside out and do the best at selling your application.

You should also have a mechanism for keeping the rest of the group informed of how your project is progressing. This might be through a formal process of having someone from your project working group meet up with your community group's regular committee to provide them with updates, or it might be a five-minute chat at the beginning of each of your regular group meetings to bring members up to date and answer any questions.

Relying on one person to do all the work is unprofessional and unfair. It isn't fair on the person with the responsibility – and it is a responsibility. Neither is it fair to the group. What happens if that person becomes unwell and is unable to carry on? How will the project continue? What happens if that person doesn't have the skills to carry out the entire project and creates financial difficulties for the group?

> A COMMUNITY GROUP PROJECT IS THE
> RESPONSIBILITY OF THE WHOLE GROUP

WHAT IS A PROJECT?

You might have an idea, but is it a project? Is it something that funding organisations will actually give money to? You will have to read the grant scheme's criteria to see if your type of project is eligible, but most funding organisations view a project as something new and in addition to your group's normal day-to-day activities. It could be something that is 'one-off' or time limited. Therefore, if you run an after-school group and you're looking for funding towards the electricity bill, or the rental cost of hiring the hall, then many funders won't be interested. This is sometimes referred to as 'revenue' or 'core-activity' expenditure, and grant funding towards this normal, everyday spending is quite rare if you've been up and running for some time.

However, if there was no after-school club in your area, but there was a demand for one (which you can prove), you might be able to get funding to help set up a group. In the same way that businesses sometimes require 'start-up' funding, community projects may need help to pay for upfront costs. After that, the community group would be expected to generate enough income to cover its future day-to-day running costs, and this sort of information would be looked at by a funding organisation. Sustainability is an important factor. No one will give you £10,000 to establish your new project if six months down the line it's going to close because of a lack of demand and finances.

Other projects that can attract funding are those which are classified as 'capital' projects. This is where a group may be looking to buy extra equipment, or refurbish a room, or build an extension. The easiest way to think of this type of project is that something 'physical' will be acquired or created. A community centre committee might discover that if they refurbished the centre to include more toilets, a better kitchen and some baby-changing facilities, then more community groups such as Parents and Toddlers, the Women's Institute, and the Guides or Scouts would book the hall and use it for their meetings. This one-off improvement could therefore generate more demand for the building and bring it back to life. However, such extensive refurbishment of the community centre is not part of the committee's day-to-day activities. It is something extra to their normal duties, which means that they might get financial help towards this cost.

Phased projects

During your search for money, you may come across projects that go through several phases and have grants for each phase. These grants might come from the same funder or they could come from different organisations. Phased projects tend to be larger projects, which are then broken down into smaller, more manageable-sized projects.

If a community centre committee wanted to add solar panels to their building to help generate electricity for use inside the hall, then this could be seen as a complete project.

However, if it wanted to add solar panels to generate electricity, and heat the water for the new shower block extension that they wanted, as well as create some new sports facilities such as a tennis court and football pitch, with associated equipment (goals, nets, balls, etc.), then this project could be broken down into smaller phased projects as follows:

PHASE 1

Installation of solar panels to generate electricity and heat water.

PHASE 2

Creation of extension to community centre to house shower block.

PHASE 3

Creation of sports facilities.

Breaking this large project down into smaller, mini-projects that are more manageable might also make finding funding easier. This is because funding organisations have their own aspirations as to which sections of the community they want to support, or what activity they wish to support. A funder with environmental concerns may be willing to help with the first phase of the project, installing the solar panels, but not want to help with the purchase of sports equipment. A sporting funder would probably be interested in providing financial support to create the new sports facilities, but not be interested in funding the solar panels. A council's community-centre grant scheme might look favourably on the extension, and even the solar panel installation, but the sports facilities may fall outside of the grant scheme's remit.

Phasing a larger project down into smaller, manageable mini-projects can make the difference between success and failure. Listen to all the advice that funders offer about phasing a project. This might be the first time your community group has tackled a project like this, but you won't be the first community group that the funding organisation has assisted with a project of this type.

BEVEL GATE GARDENING CLUB'S PROJECT

Bevel Gate Gardening Club owns some wasteland next to the community centre. A local farmer donated this agricultural land to the club. They've always wanted to create a community garden, which would give them:

- Space where members of the club and local residents could get practical experience, cultivating the land and learning how to grow a variety of plants.

- Facilities where surplus fruit, vegetable or flower produce could be sold to local residents.

- A wildlife garden, which local residents could access at all times to quietly reflect and enjoy the plant and animal life.

However, the group has never had enough money to hire the necessary equipment to clear the land and install basic services such as water and power. They've already gained planning permission for the change of use from agricultural land to leisure-and-community use, but this permission expires in two years. If they don't take action soon they'll have to re-apply for the planning permission, which is an additional cost.

Many of its members are willing to provide their time free of charge to help to clear the land and create the wildlife garden, but the club would need to hire large plant machinery and skips to clear the land, cultivate it and arrange for the local electricity and water boards to install facilities. The costs for this far exceed the funds available in the group's bank account. They had considered holding jumble sales and garden fetes to help generate some money, but by the time they would have achieved this, the costs would have risen further, forcing them to raise even more money.

The group decides at one of its meetings to look for grant funding to help it achieve this goal. A grant would help them out of this spiralling situation, and enable them to create a useful facility for the club and community.

B.
G.
G.
C.

BEVEL GATE GARDENING CLUB
CONSTITUTION

1. The group shall be referred to as the Bevel Gate Gardening Club (hereafter known as the 'group').

2. The aims of the group are to encourage and support gardeners in Bevel Gate and its surrounding area. Our objectives to achieve this are to create a varied programme of meetings and day trips, to include guest speakers when appropriate, and explore all aspects of gardening. Members will meet on a regular basis to share views and exchange knowledge and best practice.

3. Membership of the group will be open to anyone over the age of 16, living or working in Bevel Gate or the surrounding area. There is no maximum age barrier.

4. The group shall meet at Bevel Gate Community Centre on the second Wednesday of the month between 7.00 p.m and 9.00 p.m.

5. The group will be managed by an Executive Committee (hereafter known as the 'Committee') of members, who will be elected each year at the group's Annual General Meeting. Committee members shall remain in office until the next Annual General Meeting where they shall advise the Committee whether they wish to stand for a further twelve months. In the case of the resignation of a Committee member between AGMs, the Committee has the power to ask members to elect a replacement representative to undertake the role until the next AGM.

6. A General Meeting of the group shall be held annually every January to deal with the following business matters:

   - to receive and approve the Statement of the group's accounts for the previous year;
   - to receive the Chair's Report;
   - to elect members to the Executive Committee;
   - to consider any revisions required to the constitution;
   - to discuss any special matters arising;
   - to determine the membership fee for the next 12 months.

Fig. 1. Bevel Gate Gardening Club constitution.

7. The Committee shall be appointed at the AGM. Members wishing to stand for Committee positions should notify the current Chair before the AGM. At the AGM, the Chair will notify the group which position is being dealt with, which members have notified their wishes to stand, and invite the group to vote. In the event of nominees receiving equal votes, the Chair has the casting vote. The Committee will comprise Chair, Secretary, Treasurer, Guest Speaker Organiser and Competition Secretary. The Committee can create as many roles as it sees fit in order to ensure the smooth running of the group, although ideally this should not exceed a maximum of nine.

8. Each Committee position or supporting role shall be elected for the period of 12 months, until the next AGM (subject to clause 5 and resignations). It is recommended that no one person holds the same role for more than three consecutive years.

9. Committee Members will be expected to meet outside of the usual meetings to ensure that all group administration is kept up to date and to discuss future meetings of the group. For decision-making purposes, a majority vote shall determine the outcome. In the event of an equal casting of votes, the Chair shall have the final and casting vote. Where the Committee deems appropriate, a decision can be deferred until the next meeting of the group to allow the whole group to vote on the matter. Where this occurs, the Secretary should contact all members to advise them of the vote, and encourage them all to attend the next meeting.

10. The Chair shall preside at all Committee meetings and all meetings of the group.

11. The membership fee of the group shall be determined annually at the AGM and will be payable at the end of the meeting. Fees should be substantial enough to cover the costs of hiring an appropriate venue and any fees charged by guest speakers to the group. If the group invites a guest speaker who charges a higher fee than the group usually pays, an additional entrance fee may be charged to those members who choose to turn up to that meeting. Consideration can also be given to opening the meeting to the general public or other gardening clubs in the area and asking them to contribute towards costs. The membership fee should always be set at a level that does not deter people from joining the group. To assist with payment, membership fees can be paid over a period of three months if required.

▶

12. New members can attend their first meeting free of charge. Those who then wish to proceed to full membership and join the group, will pay a percentage of the annual fee as follows:

Membership starting in:	Percentage of annual fee to pay
January	100%
February	100%
March	90%
April	80%
May	70%
June	60%
July	50%
August	40%
September	30%
October	20%
November	10%
December	10%

13. A raffle will be held at each meeting. The Treasurer will sell tickets and winners of the raffle will be expected to bring in a suitable raffle prize for the next meeting. Raffle prizes should have a gardening theme.

14. The group shall maintain a bank account with Beveltown Bank to enable it to deposit membership fees and pay any expenditure that becomes due, such as room hire and guest-speaker fees. It must also ensure that at least two, but preferably three signatories are required for each withdrawal. These signatories should preferably be the Treasurer, Secretary and/or the Chair.

15. Any monies raised by the group will be used for the benefit of the group and to further its aims and objectives.

16. The group will not use surplus funds to support any political party.

17. The Treasurer shall maintain a cashbook to record all transactions and reconcile this to the bank statements as and when they arrive. A summary account of the cashbook will be provided at each AGM.

18. If the group acquires more than sufficient monies to cover day-to-day expenditure, the Committee should consider opening a savings account with their current bankers.

19. No member of the group shall bring the group into disrepute.

20. Any undesirable action by a group member towards another group member could result in the offending member being banned from the group, subject to this being the decision of the Committee.

21. The Committee shall have the right to ask a member to leave the group, if that member has contravened any of the rules within this constitution. The contravening member has the right to provide an explanation why such action was taken before the Committee makes its final decision.

22. If the Committee decides that it is appropriate to dissolve the group, it should put the matter to the group as a whole, explaining the reasons for doing so. The Committee should advise all members of the date of this meeting to encourage them all to attend and vote. If the decision to dissolve is agreed by the majority, the Treasurer shall ensure that all outstanding bills are paid. Once this has been actioned, any remaining monies shall be distributed equally between the paid-up members of the group.

This constitution was adopted by the group at its meeting of XX [date] XXXXXXX [month] 20XX [year].

Signed... (Chair)

Signed... (Secretary)

Signed... (Treasurer)

2
Finding Advice and Information

You're all fired up and ready to go. The project is a great idea, the members of the community group are excited and want to be involved and everyone's eager to get started. It must be time to start hitting the internet and looking for all of those lovely organisations that are crying out to give you some money, isn't it? Actually, no. Let's stop to draw breath for a minute and think things through.

WHERE TO GO FOR HELP

The fact that you've bought this book suggests that you're looking for some help and guidance with the grant application process. If you've never applied for any funding before, it may seem a rather daunting procedure. However, there is help out there that you can access, and it's best to start looking for it now, before you even consider developing your project idea further or applying for any money.

Local authorities or partnerships

One of the first places to turn to should be your local council. If you telephone and explain to the council's main switchboard that you're looking for community group funding, they should put you through to the right department. Alternatively, if your local authority runs a One Stop Shop or Community Services Access Point (the name varies from council to council but it's somewhere where you can make enquiries about any council service), then pay them a visit and ask for some contact names, telephone numbers and addresses.

It's quite possible that the person you end up talking to doesn't actually work directly for the council. Some local authorities have joined up with other local organisations to create partnerships, with the aim of helping local community groups to develop and improve the quality of life in their area. To the uninitiated, this may seem quite intimidating. Many individuals and community groups go about their daily lives and business without coming across such organisations. However, when you do meet them, don't let go of them! These people have a wealth of information, advice and knowledge, so grab all of the help that they offer you.

These people can have a range of job titles including:

- regeneration officer;
- grant officer;
- community development assistant;
- project development officer;
- community project development assistant.

Whatever their title is, their aim will be the same – to help point you in the right direction. They deal with hundreds, if not thousands, of requests every year and may be aware of groups like yours with similar projects. If they give you an opportunity to meet these other groups, grab it. Hearing how other groups achieved their dreams can be very beneficial.

Drawing upon their knowledge, these project development or grant officers will be able to advise you on which grant schemes are better suited to your project, as well as point out schemes to avoid because they've been oversubscribed. Occasionally, new grant schemes are launched, and it's these people who find out about them first.

People involved in project development sometimes run training days or seminars. Not only do these provide useful advice, they are also great networking opportunities. If the committee of your group isn't clear about its responsibilities when applying for funding, require clarification of the application process or need help in collating information to demonstrate the need for your project, it is these officers who may be able to come to your committee meetings to explain the details in a way that everyone can understand. Face-to-face meetings with these people can be hugely beneficial when you're starting out.

Whether you meet or talk with a project development officer from your local council or a local partnership, one of their key aims is to maximise the amount of grant money coming into your local area. Helping community groups to apply for grants from national and regional sources brings more money into your local area, all of which provides additional benefits to the local community. These are on top of the day-to-day services that the local authority provides. Whoever you liaise with, the advice that they give you, whether it is on the phone or at a face-to-face meeting, should be free of charge.

The benefit of contacting these people is that not only may they be able to provide you with details of various grant schemes, they will also be able to put you in contact with many other helpful organisations.

Voluntary sector and local development agencies

The voluntary sector (sometimes referred to as the 'third sector') has a broad definition but, for the purposes of this book, it generally includes not-for-profit groups and organisations that are not directly funded by taxes. Volunteers run many groups, although some larger organisations in this sector have paid staff. It's a sector that plays an important role in today's Britain, with many voluntary organisations providing vital services to the local community. As a result, there are several local development agencies that have been set up to help these voluntary and community groups to develop and thrive. Their role is to provide practical assistance and support to local groups, develop new initiatives which enable the sector to become better skilled, as well as providing a collective 'voluntary-sector' response to national organisations. One of these organisations that your local authority may put you in contact with is your nearest Voluntary

Action or Community Voluntary Service group. Even if you are not looking for funding, you should still make yourselves known to your local group. You can also find your nearest Voluntary Action (VA) or Council for Voluntary Services (CVS) in your local telephone directory, under the local businesses and services section (not the residential listing), or you can visit the appropriate website for your region.

England – The National Association for Voluntary and Community Action
www.nacvs.org.uk/cvsdir/ (for details of group in your area)
www.nacva.org.uk

Scotland – Scottish Council for Voluntary Organisations
www.scvo.org.uk/cvsnetwork

Wales – Wales Council for Voluntary Action
www.wcva.org.uk

Northern Ireland – Northern Ireland Council for Voluntary Action
www.nicva.org or www.communityni.org
(Note: in Northern Ireland, these support groups tend to be called 'networks' or 'community development associations'.)

If your local authority does not have a project development officer or similar either within its own staff or an associated partnership, it may be because they pay one of these voluntary organisations to provide this function on their behalf. Local authorities choose a method that is most appropriate to their local needs. Some therefore believe that these umbrella voluntary group associations are the best people to provide this facility because they have better contacts with community groups in the area. As well as providing funding advice, many also offer training on a variety of topics including:

- facilitation skills;
- fundraising techniques;
- legal issues for committees;
- how to manage a project;
- setting up a website.

In addition to this practical advice, they'll usually have a well-stocked resource centre, with books and publications covering subjects such as organisational management, and how to manage volunteers.

Some VA/CVS groups administer grant schemes themselves, which makes them useful to know! Many groups pay to access national databases of grants schemes, which is an incredible resource in itself.

If you haven't introduced yourself to your local VA/CVS or community development network then now is the time to do it. Not only will they be pleased to hear about the activities that your group gets up to, they'll be a useful resource of information and support for you. Make the most of them.

Rural community councils

Some rural parts of England have a rural community council. These tend to be county-based charities that focus on helping to improve the quality of life of rural communities, which may be disadvantaged due to their isolation. Important community services tend to be located in populated areas such as market towns, therefore people living in small rural communities can have difficulties in accessing these services.

The rural community councils are another type of local development agency and operate in a similar way to the VA/CVS groups, by offering support and advice. They too have access to grant-finding databases and may operate some grant schemes themselves. Some local authorities delegate the community project development role to their local rural community council.

To find the contact details for your nearest rural community council, visit the Action With Communities in Rural England website www.acre.org.uk, and then select 'About Acre', before clicking on 'RCC Network'. Alternatively, Action with Rural Communities in England can be contacted on 01285 653477.

Parish or town councils in England and Wales

Parish or town councils are the first tier of government in England and Wales (in Wales, they are called community councils, but should not be confused with England's rural community councils). They cover a much smaller geographical area than district and county councils, and have statutory powers to deliver a range of local services, including street lighting and looking after cemeteries or recreation grounds. Parish councils can help local community groups with project ideas either by providing space for an activity, or financially through their own grant scheme. Many also have useful communication tools that you can use to pass on information or consult the local community, such as a local newsletter or a website. To find out how your parish council may be able to help, contact the parish clerk. Their contact details might be listed under 'Councils' in your local *Yellow Pages*. Alternatively, contact your local authority, which should be able to provide contact details.

Although Scotland has similar community councils, these don't have the statutory powers that their English and Welsh counterparts have. There is no equivalent in Northern Ireland.

Regional or national bodies

Does your community group have a regional or national supporting body? Are you affiliated to a larger association? Many of these offer their own funding schemes, but if they don't they can suggest funding organisations that are interested in helping groups like yours. They may also be able to put you in contact with other groups in your area who've tackled similar projects to yours. If you're not aware of any associations, search the internet using the phrase 'national association' and the type of activity that your group is involved in. For example, a search for 'national association walking' provides links to: the Ramblers' Association and the Long Distance Walkers Association.

Your possible funder

It may well be that you've already come across the right funding organisation for your project idea. Sometimes, funding organisations promote their own grant schemes directly at the community groups they think may be interested. If your project is relatively small, you may feel that you don't need the support of any of the organisations mentioned previously. That is fine, after all the success of a project does not depend upon how many sources of help a community group consults. However, if you encounter any difficulties, make them the first people you contact. They will help out in any way that they can.

PLANNING AHEAD

With all this advice and support out there, it's quite easy to think that you can just get on and start looking for the money now. However, the chances are the advice you've been given is to go out and gather some supporting information which will form a key part of your grant application. But what sort of information do you need to find?

Have you ever seen those makeover shows on television where they transform a house from a decorating nightmare of 40 years ago into a modern-looking property? Or what about the ones where they go into people's houses and discover how dirty they are, and then transform them into clean, tidy, habitable homes? And how many garden makeover shows turn jungles into tranquil oases? The impact that those programmes achieve is that much greater because, as viewers, we see what they were like before the transformation. It's this 'before' information that is so vital to understanding the impact of the 'after' look. The same goes for your project.

BASELINE DATA

Baseline data is a phrase that you may come across when you first begin speaking with funders or grant officers about financial support. It refers to the information that shows what your current circumstances are before the project has begun. Think of it as your starting point. It is the 'before' image that will be transformed by your project. When your project is complete, it is this information that the results are compared against to assess how successful your project has been. This starting-point information is vital, so it's a good idea to collect any facts or figures, that demonstrate your current situation to your funders.

NEVER ASSUME THAT YOUR FUNDERS ARE AWARE OF LOCAL DIFFICULTIES. EVEN IF YOU END UP APPLYING FOR A GRANT FROM YOUR LOCAL AUTHORITY, TELL THEM OF THE DIFFICULTIES THAT YOU FACE. BE SPECIFIC AND CLEAR.

For some projects, your starting point can be illustrated in pictures. If your project is to clean out the local pond then take pictures of it as it is now, including the shopping trolley half-submerged in the middle and the pool of oil leaking from the rusting oil drum in the corner. The people who will consider your application may never have seen your local pond, and this helps them to put your project into context. If you're going to refurbish your community centre, take pictures of the water leaking down the walls, the buckets standing in the middle of the hall collecting rainwater and the steps at the front that don't allow disabled access.

Perhaps your project is going to promote a service that already exists? Do you run a community group that has dwindling numbers? A small publicity grant might help to raise your profile and encourage new members. Your baseline information will therefore be the number of members in your group before you began your publicity campaign.

What about tourist promotions? If you're looking to increase the number of tourists to your area or local attraction, then you need to know how many you're getting now. How else will you know whether your project has increased tourist numbers? Your local tourist information point may already collect statistics about the number of people who come through their doors. Perhaps they can let you have a copy of this information?

Don't reinvent the wheel. The chances are another organisation has already carried out some research on the topic that's of interest to you. Check out any social statistics maintained by your local authority or the Office for National Statistics, www.statistics.gov.uk, which might provide useful information from the latest census, and www.neighbourhood.statistics.gov.uk for information about your area. A postcode search will reveal statistics as varied as:

- how easy it is for people to access services;
- how far people travel to work;
- crime figures;
- health and housing data;
- general census information.

Search the internet for the websites of other national government departments, the regional development agencies, tourist boards and government agencies such as Natural England, Countryside Council for Wales, Scottish Natural Heritage, and even universities.

Demand for a project

Whilst you are gathering your baseline information together, you should also be looking at ways in which you can demonstrate to your funder that there is a demand for your project. It may be very nice to have a brand-new community centre with seating for 2,000 people and a 50-metre swimming pool attached, but can you prove the demand for those specific facilities when only 27 people live in your community?

Funders are keen to support groups who develop projects that solve a problem and meet a need. Providing evidence of that need or demand will put your project in a much stronger position. For example, a project to establish a Parent and Toddler group in the locality, which has a list of 20 parents all expressing an interest in joining, establishes a good indication of demand. If your research identifies information that the next nearest Parent and Toddler group is 15 miles away and this can only be accessed by a poor bus service that doesn't allow them to stay at the group for longer than half an hour, your argument for establishing an additional local group suddenly becomes a strong and convincing one.

When funders ask about demand for a project, they are looking for more than general comments you've heard whilst queuing up in the post office. They don't want speculation. They want hard facts.

UNDERTAKING A SURVEY

One way to find out if there is a demand for your project idea is to carry out a survey. What questions you ask and how you go about asking them is as important as answering those on your grant application.

What type of questions should you ask?

Before you begin thinking of questions, write down exactly what information you need to collect. There's no point in collecting information that you don't need and wasting time analysing it. Once you've sorted out what information you're looking for, you'll then be able to consider the best way to ask the questions.

Ideally, your survey should enable you to analyse the responses and give an indication of demand or opinions in a meaningful, numerical way. This means asking 'closed' questions or, rather, questions that have a limited response, such as 'yes' or 'no'. Closed questions might begin with 'Would you use...?' or 'Is it a good idea that...?'

Closed questions are often used to gauge people's feeling about a particular idea. The most common type that you may have come across is a statement followed by five choices ranging from 'strongly disagree' to 'strongly agree'. For example:

Table 1. Example survey question

The working week should be three days long.	Please tick
Strongly agree	
Agree	
Neither agree nor disagree	
Disagree	
Strongly disagree	

Alternatively, you may see numbers used ranging from one to five, which respondents can either tick against or circle. Or, you could ask them to rank a series of statements that you provide, using number one to identify the most important statement, down to five for the least important. Whichever system you use, it's imperative that your respondents are able to understand what is required of them.

If you're looking for ideas from people, then you need ask 'open' questions. These will begin with 'What', 'How', 'Where', 'When', 'Who' and 'Why'. For example, 'What would you like to see the land adjacent to the community centre being used for?' The problem with an open question is that it can make analysis quite difficult. If you send out 200 questionnaires, you could get 200 different responses!

Phrasing the question is therefore critical, but you shouldn't phrase it in a way that leads people to give you the answer that you'd like them to make. Remember, a survey is a tool to find out other people's thoughts, not to get them to endorse your own! If you have questions beginning with 'Wouldn't it be good if...?' then you should consider rephrasing it. It's leading the respondent to say 'yes'. A questionnaire that leads in this way does not provide true, accurate information.

Remember to use simple language in your questionnaire. You want as many people as possible to understand it, so don't use abbreviations, buzzwords or technical phrases, which may confuse. If you have to use them, explain them as clearly and as concisely as you can. Get someone else to read over the questionnaire to check for spelling and grammar. Respondents who find spelling mistakes may lose confidence in what the survey is trying to achieve.

Tell people why you want this information, and what you are going to do with it. Only ask questions that you really need answers to. Do you need to know everyone's names and addresses? If you do, you will need to ensure that your procedures for handling this personal information comply with current regulations under the Data Protection Act (www.ico. gov.uk). Would anonymous responses encourage more people to give their true feelings and thoughts? You can always give respondents the opportunity to include their name and address if they wish. Some respondents may want to be kept informed of your activities. Including returned responses into a small prize draw can also help boost the return rate.

Questions need to be answerable. There's no point asking whether people would be more likely or less likely to use new sports facilities if you haven't told them exactly what sports facilities you are referring to.

It also makes sense to think about whether you will need to carry out a survey once your project is finished. It may be the most sensible way of monitoring or evaluating the impact of your project. If so, try to formulate your questions in such a way that you can ask exactly the same question on your final evaluation survey. This will make comparing the results between the two, that much easier.

Who will complete your survey?

Think about who you are going to question. Design your

questionnaire so that it is easy to read – not everyone has twenty-twenty vision capable of reading a size six font! Today's communities are diverse, so it's important to give everyone an opportunity to respond to your survey. Find out what minority groups exist in your area. Do you need to produce your questionnaire in other languages? How will you give people who are blind or can't hold a pen an opportunity to respond? Consider including your group's contact details in case anyone has a query about a particular question.

Who is your project targeted at? If you're thinking of creating a new toy library for your local nursery group then you need to question the people who currently go to that nursery group. However, are they the only group you should question? What about the local Parent and Toddler group, or neighbouring nursery group, who may wish to join with you in developing your scheme? If you're thinking of improving your local community centre, don't just question the people who currently use it, you need to question those who don't. If you improve the centre in some way, it might encourage new people to use the facilities. Dropping a questionnaire through every local letterbox gives everyone in the local area an opportunity to respond. If you decide to stand outside the local newsagents for two hours on a Saturday morning, how are you going to obtain the views of all those local people who don't go anywhere near the newsagents on a Saturday morning?

If it's not possible to survey everyone (which for practical reasons it may not be), you need to ensure that those you do survey represent the group or type of people that your project is aimed at. There's no point interviewing schoolchildren about whether there's a demand for a local over-sixties dating agency! Likewise, if your project is aimed at the older generation, is standing outside the local youth club the best place to capture this market, or would you be better off going into residential homes and asking people your questions in a face-to-face interview?

Be patient

Give people time to complete a questionnaire, and make it easy to get the responses back to you. Do you need to include an envelope, prepaid if necessary, to encourage people to send it back? Is the manager of the local convenience store or pub willing to have a collection box for completed questionnaires? The easier you make it for people to complete and return, the more responses you are likely to receive.

Consider including a check question, to ensure that your respondent is eligible to take part in your survey. For example, if you're surveying your local community, you might want to ask for their postcode, to validate that they live in the postcode area that you are surveying. Don't include too many questions though; the shorter your survey, the more likely people are to complete it.

Analysing the results

Once you've received all of your surveys back, you need to analyse the information that has been provided. If you included a check question to validate responses, go through them all now, and remove any that don't meet your criteria. There's no point analysing information that you can't use.

Count the number of valid responses that you've received and calculate what this is as a percentage of the total number of surveys issued to give you a 'return' or 'response' rate. For example, if you issued 200 surveys and received 120 back, you achieved a 60 per cent return:

(Number of surveys returned ÷ total number of surveys issued × 100)

Now go through and collate all the information from each set of questions, and count the number of responses. Tick each questionnaire when you've finished with it so you know that it's been included in your summary. It may sound obvious, but if you don't you won't be very happy when you notice that on one question 70 people agreed with your statement whilst another 60 disagreed, and you only had 120 responses to begin with!

Summarise the response for each of your questions asked, and then look to see if the respondents agree with your ideas. If you have high percentages agreeing with your proposals, your survey now suggests to potential funders the level of support that exists for your project. If they don't, then it's time to take on board what those respondents have said and review your project. It may be disheartening, but it's better to find out now before you've put extra effort into looking for funders and ultimately delivered a project that nobody will use.

Your respondents may also be interested in the results, so consider giving them some feedback. Can you post the results on your website, or the Parish Council's website, or stick up posters at the questionnaire return points that you used? Keeping your local community informed of your progress can be just as important as keeping your community group informed.

FEASIBILITY STUDIES

For every problem, there is often more than one solution. In fact, when you're out in the local community gauging opinion of your project idea, or undertaking a survey, you may find that local community members suggest ideas that hadn't even crossed your mind. The answer may be a feasibility study.

A feasibility study analyses what the problem is, looks at the various ways in which the problem can be solved and then makes a recommendation based upon that information. It's this analysis of all of the options, sometimes referred to by funders as an 'options appraisal', which should show why your project idea is the best one for solving the problem. These studies are often carried out for much larger projects when a lot of grant money will be required. Funders want to make sure that by awarding such a large sum, the project will actually work, and solve the problem it is trying to tackle.

For many reading this book, your project probably won't be large enough to need a feasibility study. Your own research, along with any other surveys you carry out may be enough to demonstrate the need, demand and best solution for your problem. Seek advice from your local authority, voluntary sector or funder contact if you're unsure. However, if you're looking to undertake some extensive works on a local community centre, for example, you may need to undertake a feasibility study to ensure that the grant money will be money well spent. If your community centre is 100 years old, and you want to spend £50,000 modernising it, funders may consider it better value for money if you expand your project and build a brand-new community centre instead. That may mean that they will end up giving you a much larger grant, but would giving you £50,000 now be the best use of the money, if your community centre only lasts another 10 years?

Feasibility studies don't come cheap, although some funders are willing to help with these costs. A feasibility study could quite easily become the first phase of a multi-phase project. Finding the right people to undertake your feasibility study may mean advertising for consultant organisations to bid for the work. If you think you may need to carry out a feasibility study, or your funders suggest that you need one, speak with the grants officer at your local authority, or liaise with your contact at your local VA or CVS. The National Council for Voluntary Organisations publishes the *Directory of NCVO Approved Consultants*, which is updated on a regular basis, listing contact details as well as providing advice and support about the consultancy process.

BUSINESS PLANS

For some people, the phrase 'business plan' conjures up images of documents running to several hundreds of pages full of spreadsheets and other complicated flowcharts and incomprehensible data. Well, it doesn't have to be like this at all. At its most basic level, a business plan is a 'to do list'. They are also sometimes referred to as 'action plans', 'forward strategies' or 'management plans'. Essentially, they list:

- the work that needs to be done;
- when it needs to be done by;
- who needs to do it;
- any risks involved;
- whether any other help is needed from elsewhere to achieve this;
- how you will keep the project going in the future.

For many small projects, a separate business plan document won't be necessary, but if your project is looking for a larger sum of money, funders may expect to see one. However, funders will also be interested in seeing a business plan if your project is looking for a 'pump-priming' or 'start-up' grant to help get it up and running. Funding organisations will be keen to see how you will finance your project to keep it up and running once their grant money has run out.

A business or action plan that demonstrates how you will achieve this, and what action you'll take to remedy any difficulties, will give further confidence to your funders. For example, if your project is to establish a local festival, which you hope will become an annual event, you may be able to attract grant funding for the first year or two, but funders are going to want to see what ideas you have for continuing into the future without their money.

Swotting up

As well as planning ahead all of the work that needs to be done, a business plan can also have what is called a SWOT analysis. SWOT stands for:

- **S**trengths
- **W**eaknesses
- **O**pportunities
- **T**hreats

Strengths

Listing your strengths not only boosts morale, it will also help you to focus your minds when completing your application form. If your project is to establish a new festival, and members of your group have experience of working with other festivals, then that is a strength because it shows that you have some idea about the work that needs to be carried out to bring it to fruition. If you're looking to set up a toy library, and already have letters of support from prospective borrowers, that is a strength because it demonstrates that there is a demand.

Weaknesses

Nobody is perfect (thankfully!) and we all have weaknesses in our lives (you don't have to mention chocolate though), so don't expect your initial project idea to be perfect either. The challenge is to find out what those weaknesses are and then look at ways in which you can overcome them. A project that needs a large number of volunteers to clear land might have a weakness if the local population is very small. However, having identified it as a weakness, it now allows you to focus your mind on how you could resolve this. Could you see if neighbouring Scout groups would be willing to help?

Opportunities

Does your project tap into any opportunities that are currently available to you? Perhaps your local authority has just launched a grant scheme specifically to help project ideas such as yours. Might you be able to link up with other similar organisations in your area? Have other circumstances come together which mean that now is a good time to develop your idea? If your project idea is to increase the sports facilities at your local community centre, and a neighbouring farmer has offered to sell an adjacent field, then this is a great opportunity to implement your idea. It helps you to explain to funders why now is the right time for your project.

Threats

Threats could be 'future difficulties'. They may be something over which you have no control, but you still need to consider because you may need to amend your project. Perhaps the government or your local authority is considering new legislation, which may affect your project. What impact might this have, and what action do you need to take now to reduce those threats?

A simple business or action plan should consider how the weaknesses and threats can be overcome or reduced, as well as look at ways in which you can build upon your strengths and opportunities. It should then demonstrate to anyone who looks at it how you will achieve this, and what steps you need to take to implement your project. Sitting down with members of your community group to discuss how the project will proceed, identifying the specific actions that need doing, and who will do them, will make completing an application form easier. Each of these steps can be laid out in table format.

Table 2. Basic business plan/action plan layout

Target	Action required	Person responsible	Target date	Comments
What you want to achieve	What you need to do to achieve it	Who is going to do it	When do you need it done by?	Any other information you may need, i.e. support from another organisation

For many small projects, funding organisations won't want to see a business or action plan, but it's still a useful technique to help you to think these ideas through before completing an application form. Further information about business plans can be found in *Preparing a Winning Business Plan* by Matthew Record (How To Books).

BEVEL GATE GARDENING CLUB'S DOCUMENTARY EVIDENCE

The Secretary of the Gardening Club discovers that their local county council has a community grants officer, and invites them to the club's next committee meeting. The grants officer advises them to ascertain the exact level of demand for the community garden in Bevel Gate and suggests that they carry out two surveys – one to assess the level of interest from the group, the other to obtain the community's views. The grants officer suggests that they find out whether there are any local or national policies which might support their efforts, either directly or indirectly, and recommends that they produce a basic business plan to demonstrate how they will meet the cost of the water and electricity bills in the future.

At the next Gardening Club meeting, the Chairman tells the group what they've found out and asks for volunteers to help out with collating this information.

- One volunteer takes some photographs of the wasteland now, as evidence of their starting point.

- Three members create a short questionnaire to survey the community.

- Another two agree to help deliver questionnaires to all 1,603 properties in the community.

- The Secretary agrees to survey the Gardening Club's members and research for any local or national policies that might be useful.

- The Treasurer looks for similar projects on the internet to try to establish the anticipated running costs of the water and electricity utilities.

The Secretary finds a facts and figures page on the local county council website, which has data from their own surveys and the last census. According to this, Bevel Gate has a population of 2,818, in 1,603 properties, 132 of which have no access to a car. This means that they will need at least 1,603 copies of their questionnaire. It also suggests that the 132 properties without a car may be interested in purchasing locally produced fruit and vegetables. The council's website also highlights that one of its policies is to protect and enhance the natural environment whilst promoting sustainable living.

Another group member discovers that the central government department for the environment has a policy that encourages the creation of new small-scale wildlife habitats.

With this information, and the data it hopes to collect from the questionnaire, the Bevel Gate Gardening Club feels that its project not only meets a local demand but also fits in with government polices at a local and national level.

B.
G.
G.
C.

B.G.G.C.

Bevel Gate Gardening Club

Community Garden Questionnaire

Dear Resident

Bevel Gate Gardening Club owns some wasteland next to the Community Centre, which we'd like to turn into a community garden. Not only will it provide a great practical facility for those who've never gardened before, it will also have a wildlife garden for all residents to enjoy and offer fresh produce for sale. This conversion will be costly, but grant funding may help us achieve this goal. To assist us with the grant funding application process we would be grateful if you could spare a few minutes to answer the questions below. **Completed questionnaires should be returned to the post office by Monday 10 September.**

Q1. If there was a practical facility where you could learn new gardening techniques, would you be interested in using it? ☐ Yes ☐ No

Q2. If fresh fruit and vegetables were available from the community garden at an affordable price, would you be interested in purchasing some? ☐ Yes ☐ No

Q3. For part of the land we want to create a wildlife garden, with seats and benches, somewhere for the local community to come and relax. Would you use such a facility if it were available? ☐ Yes ☐ No

Q4. Which of the following would you like to see in the community garden?

Wildlife pond ☐ Fountain ☐ Raised beds for easier cultivation ☐

Tables ☐ Seats and benches ☐ Other suggestion..................

▶

Fig. 2. Bevel Gate Gardening Club Community Garden questionnaire.

Q5. If you could buy fresh fruit and vegetables from the garden, how often would you buy the produce?

Weekly ☐ Fortnightly ☐ Monthly ☐ Occasionally ☐ Never ☐

Q6. Which produce would you be interested in buying from the community garden? Please tick all that apply.

Potatoes		Peas		Cabbages		Broccoli		Leeks	
Run. Beans		Onions		Cauliflower		Lettuces		Herbs	
Marrows		Flowers		Pumpkins		Radishes		Sprouts	
Tomatoes		Carrots		Courgettes		Specify below other produce			

....

....

Q7. Would you be interested in volunteering to help with this project?
☐ Yes ☐ No

If 'Yes', please write your name and address below so we can contact you.

....

We only need your name and address if you want to volunteer.

Turn over to add any general comments you may like to make.

Please return your questionnaire to the post office by Monday 10 September. Thank you.

3
Looking for Funding

So you know what you want to achieve and you've got the constitution sorted, identified all of your background information and can prove that there is a need for your project – all you need to do now is start asking people for the money. But where exactly do you find these people?

WHERE TO START LOOKING?

It might come as a shock, but the first place you should look is close to home. What financial contribution can your group make? You're probably looking for grant funding because you don't have the resources to pay for the project yourself, but let's look at this from the funder's point of view. Which of the following would you have more confidence in: a group wanting a £5,000 grant for their £5,000 project, or one who wanted £4,500 to put towards their own £500 for their £5,000 project?

Admittedly, this isn't enough information to make a judgement on, and both projects have just as much chance of success or failure, but wouldn't you have more confidence in the group that was prepared to risk some of its own precious resources? It might not be much compared to the rest of the money required, but it does suggest that the group is taking this project seriously and, as a result, its desire to succeed will be greater.

On a practical level, many funders will expect your group to make some sort of contribution. This is where all those proceeds from your jumble sales, fetes or open days can help out. Alternatively, you may be able to draw on some 'in-kind' support. This means putting a value on the free time that your group's members give up to help implement the project, or donations of equipment that you receive. Further information about 'in-kind' support appears in the next chapter, but the important point to remember is that your first source of financial commitment should be yourselves. Some funders will even stipulate the minimum amount that they expect you as a group to contribute. This is usually quoted as a percentage of the project's total costs.

WHO TO APPROACH?

Hopefully, you've already made contact with your local council, partnership or voluntary sector support group, who will be able to point you in the direction of many funding sources. Here are some organisations, who might be of help.

Local councils or partnerships

Some local authorities offer a wide range of grants including social care and housing grants, so it's important when you contact them that you clarify that you're looking for community group funding. Contact the main switchboard, or walk into your nearest council 'one-stop shop' if you have one.

Alternatively, if you have access to the internet, try logging onto your local authority's website. The website address will be on any correspondence that you receive from them, such as your Council Tax bill, and will end with '.gov.uk' instead of the '.co.uk' or '.com' that you may usually see. If you don't have access to a computer at home, then book some time at your local library – many don't charge. Those who live in an area served by both a district and a county council should check both authorities' sites.

Searching for information on council websites has become easier following a standardisation of the main menu options on most council welcome pages. These include 'Advice and Benefits', 'Education and Learning' and 'Leisure and Culture'. The best one to look at first is 'Community and Living'. From here, you will be given a further menu from which to choose, and you need to look for phrases such as 'grants', 'community grants' or 'regeneration grants'.

You could also try using the council's search facility, but don't just type in the word 'grant'. Be specific with your search criteria. Use phrases such as:

- community grants;
- voluntary sector grants;
- regeneration grants;
- heritage grants;
- capital grants;
- sports grants.

The general theme of your project will dictate which keywords you should use. If you're looking to create a tourist information leaflet, then looking at sports grants will be a waste of time! Look for results that give you contact details of local government officers involved in the council's grant schemes, so that you can ring them up. Talking to someone about your ideas will help them to guide you to the most suitable and appropriate grant schemes.

If your local authority or partnership offers a grant scheme that is suitable for your project, then their website becomes very useful. This is because most of the scheme's documentation, such as eligibility criteria, application forms and guidance notes may be available for you to download.

Don't forget that the first tier of local government, town and parish councils may also be able to provide some support.

Local development agencies

Mentioned earlier in Chapter 2 as a useful resource for help and support, many VA/CVS or rural community councils operate grant schemes on behalf of local authorities or other funding partnerships. In addition to being a source of funding themselves, they will also have access to funding databases, listing thousands of grant-making bodies and trusts.

Charitable trusts and foundations

These vary in size from small family trusts to foundations established by some of the biggest corporate names in the UK. Whilst there are thousands of these trusts and foundations across the country, many operate using volunteers themselves. Only the largest ones have any paid staff.

Another variant of these are community foundations, which are area-based charitable trusts who administer charitable funding on behalf of other local public, charitable organisations and businesses. To find your local community foundation, visit www.communityfoundations.org.uk or use the address on p. 176 of this book.

Lottery schemes

It's not possible to list every funding organisation in the UK in this book. It would certainly be a much bigger book if it did. The organisations mentioned earlier can help you in your quest for suitable funders. However, there is one organisation which is worthy of a special mention.

Since the very first draw in 1994, the National Lottery has been raising money for charities and worthy causes. For every £1 spent on a ticket, 28p is distributed to a variety of organisations. There are several lottery funders who distribute money in the form of grants to both national projects and smaller, local community projects. Between them, these lottery funders operate grant schemes that assist projects with as little as £300, or more than £500,000, and anything in between.

A good website to visit is www.lotteryfunding.org.uk (or telephone 0845 275 0000), because this details the variety of grant schemes currently available. They do change over time, because the schemes are reviewed to ensure that the best use of the money is being made, but popular lottery-funded grant schemes have included:

- Awards for All – a scheme designed to get people together in their local community, or boost skills and creativity. Grants could be as little as £300, or as big as £5,000.

- Big Lottery Fund – designed to assist disadvantaged communities revitalise and regenerate themselves through health, education and environmental projects.

- Heritage Lottery Fund – was designed to help groups and organisations of all sizes conserve and enhance the UK's heritage, making it more accessible and increasing the public's enjoyment of it. Grant sizes range between £5,000 and over £1 million.

The lottery funding website is therefore a useful way at quickly identifying which scheme is most suitable for you and your project, wherever you are based in the UK.

Local businesses

Do you really need a grant? Might your project work if you could persuade a local business to act as a sponsor? If the national football teams succeed in getting businesses to sponsor them, why not approach a local business to see if they'll sponsor your new, under-16 football club strip?

The appendices of this book provide contact details for several grant-funding organisations, although it can only scratch the surface. Your local VA/CVS or rural community council may have access to one of the grant-finding databases that exist. Although there is a cost to the Local Development Agency for having access to these databases, most don't charge local community groups for using them.

HOW MANY TO APPROACH?

Applying for funding is very different from sending out begging letters. Don't think that a scattergun approach will mean that hopefully, at least one bullet will hit the target. Ideally, your grant application should be targeted at a funding organisation that has ideals and goals similar to those of your project. This is something you'll be able to identify from reading the eligibility criteria of a funder's grant scheme.

On a practical level, application forms can vary in length from a couple of sheets of A4 paper to several pages, so a scattergun approach would mean becoming a dedicated form-filler!

The fewer funders you need for your project, the better. It will make the administration process of claiming the grant easier and reduce the number of monitoring reports to be completed. For small projects seeking a few thousand pounds or less, one funder (in addition to yourselves) will be the most practical solution. If your total project costs £10,000, approaching four other funders to match your £2,000 contribution runs the risk of four funding organisations rejecting you. If three funders send you offer letters, and the fourth rejects you, your project will be delayed. You can't start your project until it is fully funded, so you will have to spend more time approaching other funders for the shortfall. Applying for funding takes time, which could have an impact on the existing funding that you've secured. Keep things as simple as you can.

However, there are occasions when it will be necessary to approach more than one funder. Your project may need more money than one funder is willing or able to provide. If you're looking for £30,000 and the maximum grant your local council's scheme can provide is £10,000 then you're going to have to look elsewhere.

> FUNDING ORGANISATIONS THEMSELVES MAY
> FORCE YOU TO LOOK FOR MORE THAN ONE
> FUNDER

It is quite common for funders to limit their contribution to a maximum percentage of your project costs. If a funder will only give you a grant towards 50 per cent of your costs, and expects you to cover another 10 per cent of the costs yourselves, they are forcing you to find the other 40 per cent from another funding source. Check the grant scheme's criteria to find out what the funder's maximum contribution will be.

More than one funder may be required if there are aspects of your project that not all funders will contribute towards. Think back to the phasing example in Chapter 1. An energy-saving trust may support a community group who want to add solar panels and wind turbines to their meeting place, but they won't support the general refurbishment of the building. Instead of phasing a project like this, it might be more sensible to accept the funding offer from the energy-saving trust, and find a funder willing to support the rest of the project.

Consider any advice given by the funders you approach, or project development or grant officers that you liaise with, regarding an appropriate number of funders for your project. The fewer you have though, the easier it will be to administrate.

WHERE DO FUNDERS GET THEIR MONEY FROM?

Grant-making organisations come in all shapes and sizes, and so do their funding pots. Understanding where they get their money from may also help to explain why they ask the questions they do on their application forms.

Charitable trusts

Small grant-making trusts are often created by people who have been fortunate in life and amassed a substantial amount of money, either through a family inheritance or through careful business planning and money management. Often a large sum of money is donated by that individual or family, to create a trust fund, which is then invested to generate a regular income. It is this income that is offered as grant money. With the creation of the trust fund, a group of people will then be brought together to run the trust and issue grants in accordance with their guidelines, views and ideals.

Similarly, some large corporate businesses do something similar. The Lloyds TSB Foundations offer grants in England, Wales, Scotland and Northern Ireland, and they receive a percentage of the profits before tax of the Lloyds TSB Banking Group. The same happens with the Northern Rock Foundation, who receive a percentage of Northern Rock PLC's profits. However, even though these bodies receive their money from these organisations, an independent board of trustees runs them.

Local authorities

Some local councils, parish and town councils operate grant schemes using the money they receive from the local taxpayer. The demand on this limited resource of money though often means that authorities look for other ways to fund their grant schemes.

A regional approach

Some funding organisations can only offer money as grants because they themselves have applied for it from a larger organisation. This might seem strange at first – why have a 'middle man' when the grant applicants could apply directly to the organisation that has the money? There are several reasons for this. It helps to distribute the grant money more evenly across a large area. Imagine that the government wanted to offer a grant to communities, allowing them to buy litter bins to help keep their streets clean. If the government ran the scheme themselves, they might be inundated with numerous, relatively small-value applications from one particular area in the country. This wouldn't be cost effective, and would also be unfair on those other areas of the country that hadn't applied. Instead, the government could ask local authorities or partnerships to apply for a larger sum of money and then get them to run the grant scheme on their behalf, which might distribute the money more evenly across the country.

European funding

The UK receives millions of pounds in the form of grants from the European Union. This money is given to solve specific problems, some of which aren't experienced right across the country. The decline of the mining industry, for example, led to large numbers of unemployed people in specific areas of the UK. Clearly, money was needed to help those workers retrain and gain new skills, as well as encourage new industries to relocate to those areas. However, it isn't appropriate that an office in Europe with a budget running into hundreds of millions of pounds, deals with thousands and thousands of applications from small community groups in those mining areas, asking for a few thousand pounds. It is far better for an organisation within the local community to apply for a larger sum of money, often several million, and to use this on a wide range of projects to reinvigorate the community. This could include:

- The building of brand new business parks to encourage new companies to relocate to the area, creating jobs.

- Offering new training opportunities for people to obtain new skills.

- Offering a grant scheme to community groups with their own ideas on how they can improve their lives or local area.

The type of organisation that applies for funding from either the government or the European Union in this way may include your local county, district, borough or metropolitan council, or a group of local organisations who get together to create a partnership. This partnership approach often makes sense. If Europe was offering money to improve people's health, why shouldn't the local Primary Care Trust, the social services department from your local council, voluntary groups and charities such as Help the Aged, all get together to get this money and put it to good use?

What this means is that you could be applying for a grant from an organisation that has had to apply for the money themselves! In the same way that you have to fill in an application form, they've had to fill one in, too. The only difference is that the numbers on their application form are much bigger than the ones on yours! To some this may seem a bureaucratic process and at times it is, because this is public money that has to be accounted for. However, it does enable grant money to be targeted at specific areas of a country to respond to local needs. It also means that the people you are applying to know exactly what you're going through because they've been through a very similar experience themselves. And if they hadn't applied for the money, you wouldn't have a grant scheme to apply to now to enable you to fulfil your dreams.

UNDERSTANDING A FUNDER'S PRIORITIES

Funders have their own priorities about the sort of projects they want to support. It all depends upon what their overall aims and objectives are. Projects that will produce results to further the funder's aims will therefore be of most interest to those funders. The idea behind a funder's aims and objectives is exactly the same as the reason why your community group has a set of aims and objectives as part of your constitution. They explain why you exist and what your role is.

Aims and objectives may change over time, in the same way that those of your groups can. There are a variety if reasons for this.

- **Private Trusts**. Some larger trusts make a point of changing their aims on a regular basis. Wise investment of income-generating funds means that they will have a good supply of money over the years. Instead of having a scattergun approach of helping as many groups as possible as they can over time, they might find that focusing on particular goals over a short-term period has a greater impact. Grant money is sometimes used as a pump-primer. This means that once the project is up and running, its day-to-day running costs are covered by the income it generates. A trust may find that it is better to spend two years' money on health-related projects across the entire country, and once up and running they can turn their aims and objectives elsewhere, perhaps on environmental projects.

- **Local authorities**. In the same way that we've had different national governments over the years, local politics affects the policies and goals of our local authorities. National government policies can have knock-on effects for local authorities. As a result, some of the authority's priorities will change, and some funding schemes will be dropped in favour of new schemes with new aims and objectives.

- **National Lottery**. The way the National Lottery money is used for good causes often depends upon the opportunities that arise. When the lottery was established in 1994, there were five 'good causes' which lottery money was targeted at:
  - arts;
  - charities;
  - heritage;
  - millennium projects;
  - sports.

In 1999, the new aim of 'Health, Education and Environment' was added, because after the year 2000 the next round of millennium projects wouldn't be due for some time! Lottery funding also found its way to the London 2012 Olympics.

It may seem obvious to say, but understanding what funders want to achieve with their money will save you time and effort. For example, Sport England's aim to help people start, stay and succeed in sport, means that they're not interested in your project that aims to help mature people get to grips with modern computers!

ELIGIBILITY

Your project may share the same aims and objectives of a funding organisation, but that doesn't automatically assure you of the right to some money. In addition to these common goals, funders often impose eligibility criteria. Think of these as rules that demonstrate who can and can't apply for funding.

> NEVER COMPLETE AN APPLICATION FOR FUNDING WITHOUT HAVING READ THE ELIGIBILITY CRITERIA

If your community group is a constituted not-for-profit group, and a funder's eligibility criteria states that only registered charities can apply, then you're wasting everybody's time. It doesn't matter how good your project is, if you don't fit the criteria, don't apply.

This also means that if a long time passes between you identifying a possible funder and completing an application form, take the time to obtain a copy of the latest eligibility criteria from that funder and read them through once more. Eligibility criteria can quickly change to help a funder achieve a specific aspect of their aims and objectives or when they change to new aims. So, a funder with a five-year aim to support a wide range of projects with grants between £500 and £50,000 in total may change these criteria if it discovers that, after two years of running, it is supporting three times more projects at the higher end of the funding scale, rather than the lower end. A change in their eligibility criteria stating that now only projects looking for between £500 and £10,000 can apply means that the funder is still meeting their aim of supporting a wide range of projects, but it is now focusing upon its own weakness of attracting smaller projects.

> NEVER 'TWIST' YOUR PROJECT TO MEET THE AIMS AND OBJECTIVES OF A FUNDER TO MAKE IT ELIGIBLE FOR FUNDING

If your project meets some, but not all, of a funder's aims and objectives, don't be tempted to amend your project so that it meets all of the funder's priorities. Your project's first priority is to solve your community's problem. Tweaking your project to fit the funding criteria forces you to deliver the project that meets that funding criteria, and that isn't necessarily the same as the project that you really need to deliver. If a funder suggests that amending your project will allow them to give you more money, think long and hard. Deliver the project that *you* need to deliver for *your* community.

When checking the eligibility criteria, look out for submission deadlines. Funding organisations may accept grant applications at any time of the year, or they may have fixed application submission deadlines. Establish when you can submit an application, and ensure you meet any deadlines imposed.

EXPRESSION OF INTEREST FORMS

It's quite possible that some of the support and help out there for you can assist you even further, by identifying the grant schemes that might be most appropriate for you. Whether it's your local authority, local partnership or voluntary support group, they may ask you to complete an Expression of Interest Form when you first contact them.

This will be much shorter than an application form, but it can collect enough information for them to identify possible funding organisations based upon their knowledge of which schemes are still seeking applications, which schemes share your aims and objectives, and which schemes you may be eligible for.

The questions asked will include all the usual contact information, as well as a brief description of what your project is about, the costs, an estimated timescale, what your project hopes to achieve and who the beneficiaries will be. Although many of these questions will also appear on an application form, you should understand that an Expression of Interest Form is not an application form. It can, however, be an excellent tool to help identify the right funding organisations for you, which can only be a good thing. It is still your responsibility to check that you meet the eligibility criteria of any funding organisations identified.

BEVEL GATE GARDENING CLUB'S APPROACH

With the help of the community grants officer at its local authority, Bevel Gate Gardening Club identifies two possible funders, based upon its current estimate of costs. One is a lottery-funded scheme aimed at supporting local communities to improve community facilities, whilst the other is an environmental grant scheme being operated by a local partnership, which has secured funding from several sources. Having read the eligibility criteria of both grant schemes, the gardening club feels that the aims and objects of the environmental grant scheme reflect the aims of its project better than those of the lottery-funded scheme.

The Committee decide to apply to this grant scheme, and at the next meeting of the group check that they meet the up-to-date eligibility criteria. Then they download an application form directly from the funder's website.

4
Application Forms

Once you've checked the eligibility criteria of all the funders you've decided to approach, it's time to begin completing those application forms.

GENERAL INFORMATION

Whether you complete paper forms or electronic versions, a cursory glance through all the questions might fill you with fear. Suddenly, winning the lottery, rather than applying for a lottery grant, seems much easier. However, there are some basic steps you can follow to make this process easier.

- Find yourself somewhere quiet to sit down and read through the forms. Don't even think about completing any of the questions yet. Just sit down and read through it all, so you understand what information it is that you are being asked to provide.

- Understand what you have been given. Some application forms run to several pages because they include detailed and helpful guidance notes next to each question. Other funders may enclose a set of guidance notes separately, or have supplementary question sheets for different types of projects.

- Check that the funder has sent everything they said they would. If an appendix is missing, ask for it straight away.

- Jot down notes of any points or questions you don't understand, *and then double-check the guidance notes*. The guidance notes are there for a reason, and whilst many funders are happy to deal with questions by phone, the answers to the vast majority of questions are found in the accompanying notes.

- Check whether there is a deadline by which the forms and supporting information need to be returned by. If there is, schedule a timetable with the other members of the group to allow it to be completed and checked within the timescale. Imagine what impression you will give to a funder if you are constantly ringing up to ask for extensions to deadlines. If this is how you cope with completing an application form, what impression will they have of how you will manage your project?

Application forms will vary in size and thickness from funder to funder. The questions that they will ask will also differ. However, there are several common questions that many funders will want answered to help them assess your project.

CONTACT INFORMATION

Who to contact?

Clearly, the funder needs a contact name, address, telephone number and email address of a key person in your organisation. Think carefully who this should be. It needs to be someone who knows about the project, and knows who is dealing with each aspect of it. This may seem obvious, but it also needs to be someone who is contactable! Funders appreciate that community groups are often run by volunteers who have other commitments and day jobs. Whilst staff from these funders are helpful and willing to visit community groups during the day, evening or weekend, most of the administration of grant application processing is undertaken during office hours. That doesn't mean to say that your contact needs to sit next to the phone all day in anticipation of a call (if you've completed your form properly, there shouldn't be any need for anyone to contact you), but it certainly helps the process if any queries raised by funders are answered quickly within a day or two.

Project name

Consider giving your project a title. It doesn't have to be anything fancy or creative (for example, Community Gardens for Bevel Gate, Local History Leaflet, Festival 20XX), but it helps to give your project an identity. It also demonstrates that the project is something special, in addition to your day-to-day activities, and gives the staff at the funding organisations something to clearly refer to in any communications they send to you. Hopefully, you'll consider making applications for new projects in the future, so giving each of them a title will help to differentiate between them. This is particularly important if you've decided to break down a large project into several smaller phases.

Some history about your group

Funders like to know a little bit about community groups, why they were established, how they operate, what they set out to achieve and how long they've been running. This is where they'll want to know about your registered charity number if you are a charitable organisation, whether you're part of a larger organisation and how long you've been in existence. Whilst the age of the group isn't a barrier to funding, a group that has been around for a while suggests that it has solid foundations and is well administered.

PROJECT AIMS AND OBJECTIVES

What is your project?

Be specific. Which of the following statements tells you more about what an applicant wants to achieve?

'This project will breathe new life into our community centre by refurbishing and redecorating it, thus encouraging more people to use it.'

or

'This project will rewire the community centre and install an efficient eco-friendly heating system, replacing two large electrical fires installed during the 1970s. It will also relocate three non-load-bearing dividing walls, changing our current space of one large hall and two unusable walk-in cupboards into one large hall capable of holding 150 people, and two smaller rooms, big enough for groups of up to 20 and 10 people respectively. Finally, all three rooms will be redecorated. Chairs and tables will be purchased to seat the maximum number of people in each room, whilst a computer, TV and projector, and whiteboard will be installed in the smallest room, making it suitable for training and learning opportunities.'

See how the second paragraph describes the project activities in more detail. That doesn't mean to say that the first paragraph is the sign of a bad project, but the second paragraph describes to the funder exactly what the group hopes to achieve and where the grant money will be spent. The more specific you are, the clearer picture your funder will have of what you are trying to achieve.

Why is your project needed?

This is where you need to draw upon your own research and any survey work that you carried out. It's time to give your funders all of that baseline data that you collected earlier. A project doesn't exist just because it's a good idea. There needs to be a demand for it, and this is where you have to prove it to a funder. When a community centre needs refurbishing, an empty bookings register helps to support your view that no one likes to use the facility in its current state. However, it doesn't prove that, once all the money has been spent, community groups will be fighting over themselves to start using it again. If you can get letters of support from the local community, or groups struggling to find suitable venues in your area, then this begins to demonstrate that there really is a demand.

Collect your evidence, research and other information together and summarise it on the application form. Explain to funders how you obtained your information and be prepared to provide evidence of this baseline data if a funder asks for it.

START DATES, COMPLETION DATES AND MILESTONES

Your funders will want to know when you'd like to start your project.

> *NEVER* START YOUR PROJECT, BUY ANY EQUIPMENT OR ORDER ANY WORK TO BE CARRIED OUT UNTIL *ALL* OF YOUR FUNDERS HAVE ISSUED OFFER LETTERS OR SAY THAT YOU CAN

It's therefore important that you understand how long it will take all of your funders to process your application. Having a start date of three weeks' time, when your funders take eight weeks to process an application is not practical. Why should the funders change their process to fit you?

At the other end of the scale, nothing focuses the mind better than a deadline, and all projects need a completion date. This may not necessarily be when your project comes to an end, but when all the work needed to get your project up and running is complete. Only when the community centre has been refurbished, and the builders and decorators have left, can the other community groups begin using it again. The production of a local history book may be seen by the funders as complete when it is available to buy in local shops and outlets. A festival project would only be completed once the festival is over.

However, it is not only the start and finishing dates of your project that funders are interested in. They may also want to be aware of any other key dates, or milestones, that occur whilst you go about tackling your project. Think of milestones as 'mini-deadlines' – things that must happen to allow you to continue with your project. They are the stepping stones that help you to reach your ultimate target – the end date. If you created a business or action plan, you may have prioritised specific elements of your project that need to be completed before you can move onto the next stage. It is these stages that can help you identify when your key dates or milestones are.

For example, a project to create a tourist information leaflet would need to be in the local tourist information centres for the start of the next tourist season, March. Enquiries at the printers may reveal that they need about a month to ensure that they can print and fold the thousands of leaflet that you want. The actual writing up and designing of the leaflet might take another month, but the research and taking of photos will be done by volunteers at weekends. The volunteers might have asked for three months to do this to allow them to fit it in around their other commitments. Based upon this information, your project might have the following timescale:

Table 3. Example milestones

Start date	1 October	Volunteers undertake research and take photographs.
Milestone 1	1 January	Research and information collated and typed up. Leaflet designed.
Milestone 2	1 February	Leaflet design and order sent to printers.
End date	1 March	Printed leaflets distributed to local tourist information centres.

A milestone, or key date, represents an important time during the life of your project. It can help you to monitor how your project is progressing. If it begins to slip behind schedule, a milestone or key date will bring this to your attention earlier, enabling you to take the necessary action to get it back on track. Working out what your start, key and end dates are is therefore essential, but remember to be realistic. Remember, Rome wasn't built in a day.

OUTPUTS

This is the nitty-gritty of what your project will achieve, and what funders are interested in. This gives your funders a snapshot of what their money and involvement will accomplish. Think of your outputs as the targets that your project has to achieve. Think back to those charity letters referred to in Chapter 1, where they write to you asking for money. They often provide examples of what donations will buy – £35 plants three trees, for example. So, if you were to donate £70, the output, or the result of your financial donation, would be the purchase and planting of six trees. Outputs need to be S.M.A.R.T, which means:

Specific, Measurable, Achievable, Realistic, Timely

- **Specific** means that everyone is clear exactly what is meant by the output. The output is defined well. 'An area of scrubland beautified' is not specific. How much scrubland? Where is the scrubland? What exactly is meant by 'beautified'?

- **Measurable** means that it can be quantified, and this usually means that numbers are involved. It's this aspect of your output that allows you to compare the 'before' and 'after' picture of your project. 'An area of scrubland beautified' is not measurable. How much land is in question? How do you measure beauty? An output that says '50 trees planted on two acres of scrubland' is measurable. We know exactly how many trees are needed, and what area they will cover. A measurable output means that you'll know when you have achieved it.

- **Achievable** means that the output can be completed. '50 trees planted on two acres of ground in one hour by one person' is very specific and measurable, but is it achievable? Pity the poor person who has to attempt that! Check that your targets are achievable with the funding resources that you have, and in the timescale you have to work with. Unachievable outputs do not motivate people.

- **Realistic** means using some common sense with your outputs. '500 trees planted on 20 square metres of scrubland' is specific, and measurable, and may even be achievable, but apart from looking a mess, the trees would have to be planted on top of one another and most would not survive.

- **Timely** means that there needs to be a timescale involved. '50 trees planted in two acres of scrubland' doesn't give us a timescale. When does this need to be achieved by? The planting of new deciduous trees should really take place when the trees aren't in leaf, which means during the winter period. '*50 trees planted in two acres of scrubland between October and December*' demonstrates the time aspect. However, for most of your outputs you won't need to include a specific timescale because the completion date of your project is the timescale that you will be working towards.

Outputs need to be measurable because you're the one who will be measuring them. When listing your outputs, try to think about what action you will need to take in order to ensure that you can measure and keep track of this information. If one of your outputs states that your project will offer 30 volunteering opportunities, how will you record whether you achieve this or not? Sitting at the end of your project trying to remember who turned up to help on what day isn't very practical. Yet a simple sheet of paper, where you record the volunteer's name, address, the activities they undertook and how long they helped out may be sufficient. Talk to your funder to find out what is acceptable to them.

Creating outputs can seem daunting, but it needn't be so. Some funders will provide you with a list of outputs that are acceptable to them, and you can select the ones that are applicable to your project. Funders provide support to similar projects up and down the country, so they can advise you on the type of outputs they would expect a project like yours to be creating. If you can think of an output that isn't on the list provided, ask your funder if you can use it. Some are more flexible than others are.

OUTCOMES

An outcome is something that happens because of your project. This may seem the same as its output. However, whereas outputs are very specific and measurable, outcomes look at the wider picture. Look at what you hope to achieve, and then think about the wider implications upon the local community. An outcome will be the effect or impact that your project has. The outcome of Bevel Gate Gardening Club's project to create a community garden could be:

- An increase in knowledge and skills in gardening and wildlife management.

- An improved community spirit because the community garden will give residents a new shared common interest.

- An increase in the awareness of seasonal produce through the sale of fresh fruit and vegetables from the community garden.

- An increased awareness of local wildlife issues.

What you may see from the above examples is that outcomes are more difficult to measure. Sometimes the only way to measure an outcome is to carry out another survey, because it is people's perceptions that you are trying to measure. How do you measure community spirit? Asking people if they think their locality has a better community spirit will give an indication as to how their perception of this has changed over the lifetime of the project. Outcomes are just as important because they are the wider issues that your project is trying to solve, and it's your outputs that will help you to achieve this.

BENEFICIARIES

The application form will want to know who your project is going to benefit. They don't want names and addresses, but an idea of the type of people your project is targeting. Some application forms have a tick list, and typical beneficiaries include:

- parents and toddlers;
- 16–25 year olds;
- elderly;
- people living in rural areas.

The type of beneficiaries that your project will support may well influence the funders you approach. As mentioned earlier, funders have their own aims and objectives as to who they want to support, so their list of beneficiaries may be limited to those people. Make sure that you know which people your project will be helping before you even begin to apply for funding. Your baseline information should help you to identify this, and it's something you should consider if you're going to undertake a survey.

The UK has a diverse population, and many funders are keen to ensure that their grants benefit every section of the community. As a result, you may find that funders are keen for you to identify beneficiaries within various ethnic or other minority groups.

PROJECT COSTS

The reason you are applying for funding is because there are costs involved in your project. But have you identified them all? Funders need to know of *all* your project costs, not just those that their grant money will be helping towards. If you're buying a minibus to help transport rural-living elderly people to facilities in their nearest towns, don't forget to include road tax, insurance, servicing, fuel, security, where it will be garaged overnight and any costs for adapting the vehicle. If you're buying computers for a youth group, don't forget to include the cost of software, anti-virus protection, connection and access to the internet, as well as warranty insurance.

It helps to divide your costs into the two main categories of revenue and capital. A rough guide to help remember which is which is to think of capital as one off expenditure for something physical, and revenue as day-to-day running costs. Examples include:

Table 4. Examples of capital and revenue expenditure

Capital	Revenue
Computers	Electricity, subscriptions to an internet provider, training, maintenance
Building works (new plumbing, wiring, heating, decorations, fixtures and fittings)	Electricity, gas, water, local council/ business tax, telephone bills
Sports equipment (goals, bats, balls, new pitches/courts)	Maintenance of new football or cricket pitches, such as new turf, salary contribution of maintenance staff
Toys, games, books for new toddler group	Electricity, room hire, telephone, volunteer expenses

And so the list goes on. When you're looking at the various costs, you need to be realistic. Get three quotes, if you can, to obtain a fair representation of what that cost will be. Funders will not expect you to go for the cheapest, but they will expect you to go for the right cost for your project. A higher quote providing a better quality product, or including extra 'support' that isn't available elsewhere, is a valid reason for not choosing the cheapest.

It's also worth considering supporting local suppliers if you can. Some funders may even make this a condition of your grant. This means the grant money has a double effect. As well as financing your project, it also boosts the local economy.

Keep copies of the quotes that you receive, so that you can provide them to the funders if required. Costs do vary up and down the country, and if you're applying for funding from a large national funder they may think that some of your costs are more expensive than those of similar projects they help to fund. Your quotes will back up your figures.

Once you've identified what all your costs are, add them up so that you have a total figure for all of your capital costs, a total for your revenue costs and then an overall total project cost. Always double-check your figures and addition, and, if possible, get someone else involved in the project to double-check them, too.

All too frequently, funders have to question applicants as to why the numbers don't stack up. Give those funders some confidence in your figures!

Value Added Tax (VAT)

Most community groups are not large enough to be registered for VAT purposes. This means that if a supplier charges you VAT for the goods and services that you buy for your project, you have to pay it. When calculating the total cost of your project, if a supplier charges you VAT then you need to include it in your costs.

However, some organisations, such as town and parish councils, are registered for VAT, which means that they can claim this tax back. If an invoice includes VAT, it still has to be paid, but the organisation can then claim it back from HM Revenue and Customs. Therefore, the real cost of the item is the net amount (the amount before VAT has been added). An organisation applying for funding that is registered for VAT should only include the costs before VAT when calculating the total cost of a project.

LEGAL RESPONSIBILITIES

We all have to comply with legislation, and it's important that your project does, too. If you're unsure whether a piece of legislation might apply, speak with your funder, project development or grants officer for guidance. Think how the following might influence your project:

- Disability Discrimination Act (not only should your project be physically accessible to all, but are leaflets and websites accessible?).

- Data Protection Act (what personal data will you collect? This could include information about respondents to questionnaires through to details of volunteers, or beneficiaries).

- Equal Opportunities (this includes people who want to volunteer, as well as any possible beneficiaries).

Complying with legislation can also affect your costs. If your project involves working with children, for example, anyone (paid or voluntary) will need to be checked through the Criminal Records Bureau, for which there is a charge.

PROJECT FUNDING

Now you've identified your costs, you need to tell your funder how you are going to meet them. Most funders will expect you to contribute yourself, so make it clear how much it will be and whether the money is already available. Don't be surprised if funders ask to see copies of your bank statements, proving that you have your contribution set aside if that's what you've said on your application form.

If you are applying for funding from more than one grant provider, include details here of how much you have applied for, and who you have applied to. It is also helpful to identify whether you've already had offer letters of support from any of those funders. An offer letter from another funder demonstrates that someone else has confidence in your project. If you haven't received a decision yet, try to give an indication as to when you expect to hear from them. Clarify whether any other funders on your application are only willing to support certain elements of your project. Some organisations may only be willing to contribute towards capital costs and not revenue costs. A project hoping to buy a minibus to help transport elderly people to appointments during the day and young people to social activities in the evening may find that they have to divide the costs, and therefore the number of grants required, between the funding organisation whose priority is supporting vulnerable elderly people and the other who wants to support youth programmes. If you find yourself in this position, you should always ask your funders for guidance as to how they want you to set out the information.

As you did with your project cost figures, check that your funding figures add up. Then ensure that your total project cost figure is the same as your total project funding figure. Anything different is certain to have your funders on the phone straight away! If you've asked for more money than you need, your funders will think that there are some project costs missing. If your costs are greater than the funding, they will want to know how you're going to cover the shortfall.

MATCH FUNDING

This is nothing to do with helping smokers light their cigarettes but a practice of encouraging projects to obtain their funding from a variety of sources.

It is always important to remember that grant money provided by the public sector (local councils or the government) is ultimately provided by the taxpayer – either locally, nationally or from Europe. Grant funding, like all money, is limited in supply, and therefore communities should have to demonstrate that their projects are worthy of support. This is one reason why you have to complete an application form.

A grant is not a handout that community groups should come to rely upon, so local authorities, national government and European-funded schemes sometimes stipulate that they are only willing to provide a certain percentage of the total project funding. This could be 50 per cent, 75 per cent, 90 per cent, or any figure that they decide. There are some funders who will fund 100 per cent of your costs, but these are few and far between.

So, not only have you had the joy of having to complete an application form for one funder, but you may have to go through it again to get money from somebody else. Of course, if you've completed one application form, then you will already have all the information to hand. Completing another application won't be as daunting as the first.

There is another reason why a funder might be limited in how much support they can provide to one particular project. This often depends where the funding organisation gets its money. Some grant-making bodies are in a similar position to you. They too may be an applicant who has had to fill out an application form to fund their 'project', which is the 'grant scheme' that they want to run. They have to apply to a far larger grant-making body for the money. If they are successful, they can then distribute their grant money to local community groups like yours in the form of grants. These larger grant-making bodies tend to be from the European Union or our own national government. The problem arises when different funders get their money from the same source. Are you starting to feel queasy trying to follow this? Don't panic! Let's look at an example.

Single source

Let's imagine that your project to build a children's playground in your local area will cost £20,000, and you've managed to raise £5,000 yourselves from the local community. This means that you are looking for grants to fund the difference of £15,000. Let's also assume that your local county council and your local district council have obtained money from Europe to run grant schemes specifically for youth projects, and your children's playground project fits both schemes nicely.

However, the guidance notes stipulate that they can only offer grants up to a maximum of 50 per cent of the total project costs. On the face of it, this doesn't appear to be a problem because with your local community contribution amounting to 25 per cent, you're only looking for 75 per cent of your project costs. Split this between each of the grant schemes and their individual contribution is 37.5 per cent each, which is well within their 50 per cent guidelines. You therefore apply for £7,500 from the county council scheme, and £7,500 from the district council scheme. The basic project costs and funding might look as follows:

Table 5. Project costs for example play-scheme project

Item	Amount	
Slides, swings, roundabouts and climbing frames	£17,500	
Erection of equipment, installation of safety surface (bark chippings)	£2,500	
Total costs	**£20,000**	

Table 6. Project funding for example play-scheme project

Funder	Amount	
Applicant/local community	£5,000	
County council grant scheme (secured)	£7,500	
District council grant scheme	£7,500	
Total costs	**£20,000**	

On the face of it, everything looks fine, all the figures add up and the costs and funding figures agree with each other, too. Now imagine that you'd already heard from the county council scheme and they had agreed to offer you the full £7,500, and now you're waiting for the decision from the district council scheme.

However, because both the county council and the district council have obtained the money for these grant schemes from the European Union, they need to ensure that they don't break their own grant conditions. When the district council looks at your application, and notices that you've already been granted £7,500 from the county council, the restrictions imposed upon them by their European funders mean that they can only offer you £2,500. They will have reached their decisions as follows:

Table 7. Funding shortfall caused by both funders obtaining money from same source

Total project costs	= £20,000
50% of costs eligible under European grant scheme	= £10,000
Less the part of the project already funded by European money (the county council grant scheme)	= £7,500
Balance, and amount district council can offer	= £2,500

As the group can now only get £10,000 in total from these grant schemes, they are now left with a £5,000 funding shortfall, because their project funding table now looks like this:

Table 8. Project funding shortfall

Funder	Amount
Applicant/local community	£5,000
County council grant scheme (secured)	£7,500
District council grant scheme	£2,500
Total funding secured	**£15,000**
Total costs	£20,000
Funding shortfall	**£5,000**

To avoid this happening to you, always listen to any advice that you're given when project development officers and support staff suggest grant schemes to consider approaching and who to avoid. And don't be afraid to ask funders where they get their money!

IN-KIND SUPPORT

There are some people out there who may be willing to help with your project. They might offer to give up some of their free time, or perhaps lend you a piece of special equipment free of charge. Whilst this help may be free to you, it does still have a value. And with the agreement of your funding organisation, you can use this value to count towards your own contribution to the project costs.

Volunteers

A popular source of in-kind support is the use of volunteer time. Not only can it increase the value of your group's contribution to the project, but it can also reduce costs and provide you with a project output. (Some funders will allow you to include the number of volunteering opportunities as an output.)

Bevel Gate Gardening Club will need to clear its land of any debris and loose stones before contractors get to work and lay the infrastructure for the watering and electricity points. Landscaping companies will clear the ground – at a price. By asking for volunteers from the local community to carry out this work, the need to use a landscaping company can be eliminated. That's one less cost and invoice to have to worry about. However, these volunteers will be giving up some of their precious time to do this work, and some funding organisations are willing to recognise this. To put a value on it, you need to know the hourly rate that is acceptable to your funder.

So, if Bevel Gate Gardening Club has five volunteers each spending six hours on one day clearing the land, that's equivalent to 30 hours of volunteer time (five volunteers × six hours). If a funder agrees to an hourly rate of £10, then those 30 hours at £10 per hour is equivalent to £300. That £300 can be included in the income and expenditure sections of your project. What does this achieve? Surely, by including the figures on both the income and the expenditure sections, they merely cancel each other out? Well, the 'in-kind' contribution is included in the funding section under your own contribution, and this increases your total contribution when expressed as a percentage of the project funding. When funders insist that your community group make a minimum contribution, they usually express this as a percentage, e.g. 10 per cent. This 'in-kind' contribution can therefore become very important.

Let's imagine that in this first example Bevel Gate Gardening Club can't find any volunteers to help clear the land. Its basic costs and funding might look as follows:

Table 9. Project costs before in-kind support

Item	Amount
Clearing the land	£300
Installation of utilities	£3,200
Total costs	**£3,500**

Table 10. Project funding before in-kind support

Funder	Amount	Percentage
Applicant contribution (cash in bank)	£200	5.71
Grant funder	£3,300	94.29
Total funding	**£3,500**	**100**

Clearing the land is still a cost to the group, because if they don't have any volunteers to do it, they have to pay for the work to be done. This is why it appears in the project costs.

Looking at the funding breakdown above, the applicant's contribution of £200 is just 5.71 per cent of the total project costs. So, if the grant funder was insisting on a minimum group contribution of 10 per cent, this £200 contribution isn't enough. However, if they could get volunteers to carry out the work, the funding package would change as follows:

Table 11. Project funding after in-kind support

Funder	Amount	Percentage
Applicant contribution (cash in bank) Applicant contribution (in-kind support)	£200 + £300 = £500	5.71 + 8.57 = 14.28
Grant funder	£3,000	85.72
Total funding	**£3,500**	**100**

The total project costs are the same, so the total funding required is the same. But the applicant's contribution has risen from £200 in total to £500 in total. This is an increase from 5.71 per cent of the total costs to 14.28 per cent. Despite the percentage of the applicant's contribution increasing, the actual amount of money they have to find from their bank account remains the same, at £200. However, they now exceed the minimum contribution figure of 10 per cent that the funder expects them to make.

Notice too, though, how the funder's contribution has dropped from £3,300 to £3,000. This is because the volunteers have cleared the ground free of charge, so there is no need to pay a contractor. This means that less grant money is required for the project overall.

Where's the catch?

It seems like a win-win situation, and it is, but there are limits. Some funders will limit the maximum amount of in-kind support a project can use. You should also bear in mind that you'll need accurate records detailing the names and addresses of each of the volunteers, a record of the number of hours they volunteered for, and then their signature confirming that they actually volunteered for those hours. If the documentation isn't right when you make a claim, the funder won't pay out. Some funders may provide example forms that you can photocopy and use.

Funders scrutinise volunteer time because there's a possibility that it can interfere with the percentage of the group's contribution adversely and, if left unchecked, could allow a group to make a profit! Further information about the documentation can be found in Chapter 9.

Hourly rates vary from region to region, and funder to funder, so always check these out before calculating what they may be worth. It also depends on the skill of the volunteer and the work they are doing. A community centre looking to add an extension to its building might want to use an architect in the locality who offers their services free of charge. The funder might allow you to use the hourly rate that the architect normally charges, or they may have a professional rate of their own that they'd like you to use.

Volunteer expenses

Attracting volunteers can be difficult, and one way that can help is by offering to pay volunteers for any expenses they incur whilst volunteering. For example, if you don't have refreshment facilities available, but there's a café nearby, you could offer to cover the cost of any drinks they order. However, the costs must be reasonable and only cover their expenses. As soon as volunteers start making a profit out of volunteering, they are no longer volunteers, and it's no longer in-kind support! The local CVS or your funders should be able to offer advice if you find yourself in this position.

Equipment

In-kind support can also work with the provision of equipment, whether it is donated to the project or hired and not charged for. It will still be necessary to obtain invoices for these items, but the invoices will need to make clear that they do not need to be paid. The invoices are required to ensure you claim all the grant money you are entitled to, and this is explained further in Chapter 9.

The benefit of in-kind support is that it increases the percentage of your overall contribution to the project. Where funders insist that applicants provide a minimum percentage of the funds themselves, this in-kind support can make all the difference.

APPLYING FOR FUNDING FOR MORE THAN ONE YEAR

For the vast majority of projects that this book is aimed at, funding will only be required for the short period that it takes you to complete your project. Even if you're tackling a larger project, such as the refurbishment or extension of a community centre, where the work may take longer than a year to complete, the funder will have allocated your grant from their budget for one particular year.

Projects that need staff to run and operate them may need funding for more than one year. There are funders who are willing to consider salary costs and the associated costs of running an office for a two- or three-year project. Being offered a grant for the first year does not guarantee you a grant for years two and three, but if you deliver what you promise in your first year, you will certainly be in a stronger position for your second-year application.

Always keep costs and income realistic for multi-year funded projects. Don't put the same figures down in your project-cost columns for years two and three, and then add a bit on for inflation. The costs in year one are usually greater because of set-up costs. It costs money to advertise for staff, so recruitment costs need to be included in year one, but hopefully won't be needed in years two and three. The employee will need a computer, which you'll buy in year one, but the cost won't be required in years two and three. When the time comes to fill out your application for a second year's funding, you should base your costs on the actual expenditure that you've incurred so far during the first year. (If you're applying for funding for a second year, you'll probably have to submit an application several months before the end of the first year of the project.)

You may have calculated originally that the telephone bill for the first year might be £200, but if you've only spent £40 in the first six months of year one, you need to have a good explanation as to why you've put £200 down as the figure for year two. When funders look at your application for funding for years two and three, they have much more information to hand about your project. They know exactly how much you spent because of how much grant money you've claimed so far.

REFEREES

Some funding organisations ask a referee to countersign your application as an additional check that your group is who you claim to be. This is usually someone who has known your group for some time, but is not a member, nor will they benefit directly from the grant. Funders who ask for this usually provide examples of who might make a suitable referee.

CHECKLISTS

At the end of an application form, you may find a checklist. It's an opportunity to review your application and ensure that you are submitting all the information and supporting documentary evidence that you need to. Don't think that it's there for all those other applicants and miss it out yourself. What makes you so special? Go through the checklist and ensure that you are including everything that applies. If you are unsure whether an item on the checklist refers to your project, contact the funder for advice.

THE CHECKLIST IS THERE FOR EVERYONE

It is difficult for funders to appraise a project if they don't have all the information to hand. The checklist is designed to avoid this. If a funder has all the information they need, your application may be quicker and easier to appraise, which means that you'll know the outcome of your application sooner. The checklist therefore benefits you, just as much as it does the funder.

If the checklist asks for something that you don't have available, such as bank statements, or a copy of your latest set of accounts, don't put a tick in the box and then scribble next to it 'to follow in due course'. Wait until you have all the information together and submit it complete. Funders are awash with paperwork, and the chances of a set of bank statements sent two weeks afterwards meeting up with the application form are greatly reduced. It's called a checklist for a reason. Check it – don't avoid it.

DECLARATION

The community group's authorised signatory should then sign the form after reading the declaration, confirming that the information contained within it is true and accurate. Knowingly including false or inaccurate information is fraud. Not only will funders reclaim any grant monies paid out, they may consider legal action.

The Bevelshire Partnership

BEVELSHIRE PARTNERSHIP
ENVIRONMENTAL GRANT SCHEME

Please complete every question on this form, referring to the separate guidance notes for help and advice.

APPLICANT DETAILS

Project name: Bevel Gate Community Garden Project

Community group: Bevel Gate Gardening Club

Contact name: Mr R. Weed

Contact address: Bevel Gate Gardening Club, c/o The Grass Cuttings, Bevel Gate, Bevelshire BV12 1VB

Contact telephone number: 01657 943048

Contact email: rweed@bggardeningclub.co.uk

Position held in community group: Chairman

What does your group do? Through regular meetings, Bevel Gate Gardening Club allows members to increase their knowledge about growing all kinds of plants (vegetable, floral and arboreal) to enable members to get the most from their own gardens, or a greater understanding of plants for those without their own plot of land. We regularly invite guest speakers to pass on specialist information and arrange trips to gardens of interest.

When did your organisation begin meeting? 1984

What is your organisation's legal status? We are a constituted, not-for-profit, community group of likeminded individuals

Do you have a registered charity number? No

Is your organisation affiliated to any other group? No

Fig. 3. Bevel Gate Gardening Club application form.

When do you plan starting your project? Beginning of January 20YY

When will your project be complete? End of February 20YY

Why have you chosen these dates?

Some vegetables and plants can be planted directly into the ground at the beginning of spring, for harvesting in summer and autumn. Having the project completed by the end of February allows us to make maximum use of the growing season ahead, and create the wildlife garden with least disturbance to existing wildlife in the area.

Please provide a brief description of your project:

The Bevel Gate Community Garden Project aims to clear and level the 1,750 square metre site of wasteland that we own (through a generous gift from one of our members) adjacent to the Community Centre. At present (see photos), the land is overgrown with weeds and has several large earth banks. Once the land has been cleared of weeds and levelled, the topsoil will be removed to a depth of 3 feet and replaced with new topsoil. Water and electricity supplies will then be installed. The site, which is 25 metres wide by 70 metres long, will then be split into two sections – each of 875 square metres. The first section will be laid out for growing vegetables and flowers to be used by the group and local residents as a practical area for broadening knowledge of gardening techniques. There will be some raised beds for use by less able community members. The fruit and vegetable stock produced will be sold to the local community, giving them access to keenly priced, organic, fresh produce. The second section will be used to create a wildlife garden for enjoyment by the whole community at any time. There will be seats and benches, a wildlife pond and habitat area created, with paths exploring the area wide enough to cope with pushchairs and wheelchairs.

What demand is there for this project?

A questionnaire was delivered to all 1,603 properties in Bevel Gate, of which we received 962 back, a return rate of 60 per cent. Fifty-one respondents said that they would be interested in joining the Gardening Club if we had this practical facility of being able to grow

▶

81

our own produce. Eighty-two respondents told us that they would welcome a new source of fresh produce in the village. Six hundred and twenty-nine respondents liked the idea of a community wildlife garden facility that they could sit and relax in. The Gardening Club currently has 183 members, and in a separate survey 148 expressed an interest in having a practical facility where they could develop their gardening skills. Of those 148 respondents, 23 don't have a garden of their own and would relish the opportunity to put their new practical gardening skills into practice.

Does your project link in with other projects or local/national strategies and policies?

The local authority has a policy to protect and enhance the natural environment whilst promoting sustainable living. Our project helps to deliver both aspects through the creation of the wildlife garden and the production of our own fruit and vegetables. The government's environmental department has a policy of encouraging the creation of small-scale wildlife habitats, which our wildlife garden will help to deliver.

What environmental impact will your project have?

The site is currently an eyesore, overgrown with weeds and unkept. Turning it into a usable community garden will improve the area aesthetically. The community garden and in particular the wildlife garden will provide an environmental focus throughout the year. Studies by students at the University of Bevelshire have shown that the wider the range of plants found in a garden, the wider and more diverse the range of insects and butterflies it supports, because of the varied habitat. We envisage that the heavy plant machinery needed to clear and level the site will produce a lot of noise. We aim to reduce this affect by using the machinery at weekends only between 10 a.m. and 4 p.m. The topsoil that is taken away will be recycled by a local building company, and the replacement topsoil supplied by a reputable, environmentally sustainable source.

Have you received grant funding before? No, this is our first application for grant funding.

Who will benefit from your project?

This project benefits the Gardening Club members and the local community of Bevel Gate. Up to 190 people (148 members and 42 other locals) will benefit directly from the practical facility the community garden will provide, although any of the residents can join us for specific learning opportunities (there will be no charge for attending our practical sessions, although we hope residents will consider joining our group as members). Twenty-three members of the Gardening Club without a garden will benefit from having access to a garden facility where they can hone their practical gardening skills. Residents, particularly those without a car, will also benefit because the fresh fruit and vegetables produced will be offered to them for sale, reducing the need to travel to the nearest supermarket. All of the residents, of which 629 expressed a strong desire to see such a facility, will benefit from the creation of the new wildlife garden.

Please identify which of the following outputs you will be able to achieve, and quantify a target to aim for:

Number of new community facilities created	2
Number of additional people using new community facility	629
Number of volunteers directly involved with the project	25
Number of people given access to new learning opportunities	190
Area of land enhanced	1750 sqm

Please list the outcomes of your project:

1. Increased knowledge and skills in gardening and wildlife management.

2. Improved community spirit – community garden will give residents a new shared, common interest with each other.

3. Increased awareness of seasonality of produce through the sale of our own community garden produce.

4. Increased awareness of local wildlife and environmental issues.

▶

PROJECT MANAGEMENT

Who will have overall responsibility of the project?

Mr R. Weed, Chairman of the Bevel Gate Gardening Club will oversee the project along with the Club Secretary, Club Treasurer and four other volunteers from the group.

How will the project be managed?

The Chairman, Secretary, Treasurer and volunteers will meet weekly to ensure project is progressing as planned and to discuss any problems. The Gardening Club will be brought up to date at the beginning of its usual monthly meeting. Various members of the Gardening Club, who will all be overseen by the Club's Chairman, will undertake specific jobs. A member of the project committee will coordinate the volunteers for the ground clearance, and the Treasurer will deal with all financial transactions.

What are the milestones for this project?

Milestone	Target
1st weekend in January 20YY	Volunteers clear excess undergrowth from site.
2nd weekend in January 20YY	Site cleared using hire equipment, old topsoil removed.
3rd week in January 20YY	Electricity and water companies install services.
3rd weekend in January 20YY	Replacement top soil delivered. Volunteers begin creating community garden infrastructure – raised beds, wildlife pond and pathways. Boundary fencing erected around community garden perimeter.
4th weekend in January 20YY	Gardening Club storage shed erected.
1st weekend in February 20YY	Complete hard landscaping.
3rd weekend in February 20YY	Communal garden equipment purchased.
4th weekend in February 20YY	Wildlife garden planting completed.

Please give a detailed estimate of the costs involved in implementing this project.

Expenditure item	Cost
Hire of rotavator, skip and earth mover for two days (in-kind).	£500
Removal and disposal of topsoil.	£300
Installation of electricity and water supplies.	£2,500
Replacement topsoil.	£2,000
Shed for tool storage, and produce sales.	£500
Seats, benches and paving.	£500
Plants and seed.	£500
Communal garden equipment (extension leads, hosepipes, basic tools, wheelbarrow).	£150
Boundary fence and gate.	£1,200
Volunteer time for ground clearance, topsoil removal, landscaping of wildlife garden and erection of shed. Max 100 hours @ £9 per hour (in-kind).	£900
Total	**£9,050**

Please list all of the funding for this project, including other grants applied for but not yet secured.

Funding	Amount
In-kind equipment hire	£500
In-kind volunteer time	£900
Bevel Gate Gardening Club contribution	£1,500
Bevelshire Partnership Environmental Grant Scheme	£6,150
Total	**£9,050**

What happens when your project is complete?

The money raised by selling the fresh produce will cover the running costs of the electricity and water bills, as well as general maintenance costs that will be incurred. The income will ensure the sustainability of the project in the long term.

▶

I accept that the information contained on this form is a true and accurate reflection of our project and understand that knowingly applying for grant funding using false information is fraudulent and could lead to prosecution. I understand that you may ask for any additional information during the appraisal process.

Signature .... Date ..... /..... / .....

Who should grant payment cheques be made payable to:

Bevel Gate Gardening Club

Please ensure that you have carried out all of the actions and included all extra documentation required, by placing a tick in the corresponding box.

Required	Tick
Have you completed every question on this application form?	✓
Please include a copy of your group's current constitution.	✓
Please include copies of your up-to-date bank statements – covering the last six months.	✓
Please include copies of three quotes for each item of expenditure listed in your project costs.	✓
Please include copies of written offers of in-kind support.	✓
Please include copies of offer letters received from other funding organisations if applicable.	✓
Please include copies of any planning application approvals if applicable.	✓
Please include calculations of the amount of volunteer time required for your project.	✓
Please include example of any surveying questionnaires you created to assess the level of demand for your project, and the summary of your results.	✓
Please include copies of any strategies or local policies that your project links with.	✓
Please include any maps or plans detailing your project.	✓

This information will be held on a database to enable the Bevelshire Partnership to administer your grant effectively. This information will only be shared with the funding organisations of the Bevelshire Partnership who are: Bevelshire County Council, Bevelshire Primary Care Trust and The Region Development Agency.

Please return this form to:
The Bevelshire Partnership
Bevelshire House
Beveltown
Bevelshire
BV1 1TN

5
What an Appraiser is Looking for

After all your hard work and efforts, the time will come when you have to hand over the dreams and aspirations of your project to the people who, hopefully, will allow you to make them happen. That's when the funders go off to a quiet corner and start pulling your application apart.

Actually, that's not quite true. Funding organisations are keen to spend the money that they have allocated in each financial year. The more grants they award, the more communities they can support. Think back to the situation earlier, where an organisation such as a local authority has applied for European or national government funding in order to run a grant scheme in their area. They too will have outputs to achieve and targets to meet concerning the number of projects supported. Privately funded foundations and organisations set themselves goals and targets to aim towards in an attempt to make a difference with their money.

CONTROLLING PROCEDURE

It might come as a surprise, but the people from whom you are asking for money do actually want you to succeed. They need you, just as much as you need them. However, as with all money, there comes responsibility, and the funding organisations can't just throw it around at projects that they take a liking to. There needs to be a controlling procedure, which gives proper consideration, to ensure that the money they award is given to projects that will succeed and make a difference. This process also allows the funding organisation to judge how your project will help them to achieve their aims. This is why there is an appraisal process, where every application is judged on its own merits.

INITIAL CHECKS

One of the first tasks the funding organisation will do is check that your project meets the criteria for that grant scheme. If you're not eligible, then there is no point in considering the application any further. The checklist will be consulted to ensure that all the supporting documentation has been supplied and then the application form itself will be scrutinised for any unanswered questions. Any figure work may be examined to see if the numbers add up and agree with one another.

Appraising a project involves human judgement. There are so many variables to take into consideration that a project application couldn't be credit scored in the same way that a credit card application is credit scored by a financial institution. So what sort of factors is the appraiser looking at?

Basic information

After checking your contact details, reading about your group's history and getting to grips with what your project is all about and hopes to achieve, the appraiser will begin to consider whether you are the best group to carry out the project. 'But it was our idea!' you cry. True, but that doesn't mean that another group or organisation wouldn't be better placed to carry out the project. The chances are you will be the best people to do the job, but the appraiser will consider whether the project could be delivered more efficiently by another organisation such as a local charity or the parish council. Does your local authority have a legal obligation to provide the service that you want to offer, or could an existing organisation deliver it at a cheaper cost? Do you have the necessary skills and experience to run this project?

Project costs and funding

After checking that all the figures add up and agree with one another, the appraiser will then look at them more closely. Are they realistic? This is where they may check your quotes to see how you've arrived at the figures. The chances are your project isn't unique. Appraisers come across many similar projects, so they have an idea of the sort of costs they would expect a refurbishment, festival or training project to incur. They will also check that you've allocated the expenditure to the right category of capital or revenue. If a funder is only prepared to fund capital expenditure, they will ensure that you haven't included any revenue expenditure. They must adhere to their own guidelines in order to treat all applicants fairly and equally.

When examining how your project is funded, they'll check that your contribution meets their minimum requirement, and they'll also look at who else you've approached for funding. Have you asked all the right people? Projects promoting sport would be expected to target funders with an interest in the delivery of sports. If you have approached a variety of funding sources and received rejection letters, include copies of these rejections in your application; it demonstrates to an appraiser that you have considered other funding options.

The appraiser will also obtain a rough indication as to when in time you will need your money. The building of an extension on a community centre may need a large proportion of the grant money halfway through the project to pay for the major building works, with the remainder needed towards the end when the minor internal redecoration is undertaken. An applicant's own contribution may be large enough to pay for the first phase of a project. Some funding organisations try to identify when projects will claim money so that they can ensure that they have it available.

Outputs and outcomes

If a funding organisation provides a list of acceptable outputs, the appraiser will examine the outputs listed in your application to see if you've identified the right outputs for your project, and whether they are realistic. If you claim that there will be 400 volunteers helping with your project and there are 400 people living in your community, the appraiser will question whether this is achievable. Don't forget they have other projects to compare yours against. They will also examine how you will measure your outputs. If you're creating a tourist leaflet to encourage more visitors to your local area, how will you know how many more tourists are coming because of your leaflet? The appraiser will be looking at the system you'll put in place to record this information.

Start, completion and milestone dates

Do your dates stack up? An appraiser may question why your project to clean out the village duck pond and enhance the village green begins in spring, when animals may be nesting and needing to use the area. It would be much better to leave it until late autumn when disturbance to the area can be kept to a minimum. Have you allowed for any periods of holiday? It can be very difficult to get work done during the week between Christmas and New Year, for example. Does your project need planning permission? Have you asked your local authority what the average processing time for planning applications is? Getting this date wrong could severely affect your whole project and all future dates. Your keys dates, if realistic, will help a funder decide when you are likely to require your grant money, which will enable them to ensure that they have the money available at the right time.

LINKS WITH OTHER PROJECTS

This may seem strange but some funders will consider whether your project links in with any others in your area. For example, if a funder has awarded a grant to a further education establishment in your area to encourage women to retrain after being out of the workplace for several years, your project of providing crèche facilities neatly complements this. By providing the crèche facilities, more women will have the time to undertake a training course at the further education centre. Your project may help to maximise the benefits of the grant funding for the other project, assuming that you can demonstrate a demand from young mothers who want to return to work but need childcare facilities whilst they retrain!

LINKS WITH LOCAL, REGIONAL OR NATIONAL STRATEGIES

Local authorities, regional organisations and national government regularly produce strategies for improving our lives. They range from ways to educate children, ideas to reduce crime and thoughts on promoting entrepreneurship through to guidance on improving access to services, or improving the health of the nation. Identifying a link with one of these strategies may help to strengthen your evidence-of-need argument. If, for example, the national government has a strategy to increase the number of sporting opportunities for children of school age, and your project is to improve the local sports facilities for after-school sports clubs, it's another argument to an appraiser that you are meeting a need. You still need to demonstrate that there is a demand for those facilities in your local area, but if that particular government strategy is helping to create that demand, a funder may look more favourably on a community group that has ideas on how to solve that demand problem.

If one of the funders you are applying to is your local authority, find out what their core aims and objectives are, and then look at how your project may help to achieve those aims. If your local authority wants to ensure that children have safe and easy access to a range of play activities, an appraiser of the local authority's grant scheme will be interested in your project to provide and install a new children's playground in your local community. It doesn't guarantee that you'll get the grant, this is just one of many aspects the appraiser is considering, but obviously, the council's grant schemes will be keen to support projects that share the same visions and goals as they do.

RISK ASSESSMENT

These days it doesn't seem to matter what you do in life, there is an element of risk attached to it. The same goes for projects. Not only is there a risk that the project might fail, there is also a risk that the project might not deliver all of the outputs and targets that it sets out to achieve. This might be due to external influences purely beyond your control. And whilst you can't guarantee that the sun will shine on your street party or festival, or that all of those 50 people who offered to volunteer will actually turn up, an appraiser will be looking to see what actions you will take to reduce the risk.

An application form may specifically ask a community group to identify the risks that might arise during the project, and how they will overcome them. An appraiser will consider whether all the main risks have been identified, and whether the steps taken to reduce the risk are appropriate.

FORWARD STRATEGY

It sounds rather grand, but when an appraiser looks for a forward strategy what they want to know is, what will happen to your project when all the grant money has been paid out? When funders award money, they're looking for a lasting impact. It's no good enhancing an area of scrubland with new plants and shrubs if no one is going to take on the responsibility of tending to them. What's the point of providing money for a new community centre if there isn't a plan to promote it and its facilities to encourage people to come and use it? What happens when all the toys purchased for a children's toy library at the local nursery are broken? Is there a plan to repair or replace toys as they become damaged? If so, who will pay for them? You could make a small charge every time a toy is borrowed. How will you keep this money separate from the group's other funds to ensure that it isn't absorbed into the group's day-to-day running costs? Show your funders that you have thought about what might happen when your project is complete.

VALUE FOR MONEY

No, appraisers are not looking to buy two projects for the price of one – well not quite – but they are aware that their grant money is a very limited resource. If they awarded money to all the groups who applied, they'd often be giving away their entire grant budget several times over. So the money that they offer to projects has got to work hard. It should achieve what it sets out to achieve.

This does not mean that the appraiser is looking for you to use the cheapest suppliers available. We all know that you pay for what you get in life, so cheap doesn't always translate into long-lasting. A similar product which costs 10 per cent more, but comes with a warranty lasting five times longer, may well be money better spent when looking at the overall cost of a project over its lifetime.

The appraiser will also look at how your costs compare against those of a similar project. Not only will they look at the costs, but they'll also compare the outputs. If one project managed to plant 300 trees for the price of an £800 grant, why is another project only planting 200 trees with a £700 grant? Think back to those charity letters you get through the post. If you had £50 to donate, are you going to give it to the charity that can use it to create three metres of new footpath or the one that will use it to create two metres of footpath? This is another reason why you should maximise the number of outputs you can claim for your project.

Should someone else do it?

Value for money doesn't just cover the obvious financial side of your project. Appraisers will look at the similarities your project has with others in the area, how you link in with these, and whether anyone else can deliver your project better. If a parish council were to apply for a grant to enhance the village pond, an appraiser will consider whether they are the best people to deliver the project. Would the local Wildlife Trust, who have had grants from them before, be better placed to do it? That's not to say that a parish council can't tackle the project. They would probably do a very good job. But could the Wildlife Trust, who have experience in this type of work, be able to do it more effectively? The parish council, for example, might need to hire the tools to do the job. The Wildlife Trust may already own them. Straight away there is a cost saving – there's no need to hire the tools. The end product will be the same, but without the need for quite as much grant money.

Some grant schemes allow community groups to apply for sums as small as £300 or as much as £50,000. If an appraiser sees that a project can be achieved for £600 less grant money, it means there may be an opportunity to help two additional community groups who are looking for small £300 grants. Value for money isn't about cutting costs, but maximising the number of community groups like yours that they can help.

OPTIONS APPRAISAL

Whatever we do in life, we generally have a series of choices open to us. If we want to buy a newspaper, there is a wide range that we can choose from, whether they are local, regional, national, daily, weekly, highbrow or something in which to wrap up your fish and chips. The same applies to your project. Having identified a need for your project, are you sure that you've chosen the right solution for this problem that you are trying to solve? Is applying to the funding organisation for financial support the only option that is available to you? This is why funders sometimes ask groups seeking larger sums of money to carry out a feasibility study. If this happens to you, remember that you may be able to get grant funding to cover this cost.

An options appraisal is not an easy way for funders to reject projects. They are keen to support you. However, this stage considers what other opportunities are available to you. If you've identified some of these in your application, and then explained why you've chosen this application as the option, your appraiser will see that you have seriously thought about all of the ways that your project could have been developed. If you've carried out a feasibility study, summarise the contents on the application form, but offer to send a copy of the full study to the funder, if they want to see one. Options that an appraiser may look at include:

- Are you the best people to deliver this project?
- Is now the right time to be setting up the project?
- What happens if a funder only agrees to fund part of the project?
- Would it be better to link up with another similar project in the area?
- Where is the best place for this project?

ENVIRONMENTAL IMPACT

There are two aspects an appraiser will look at here:

- How environmentally friendly the project will be when up and running.
- What the impact on the local environment will be during implementation.

We all need to think more about the consequences of our actions on this planet, and funding organisations have realised that they too need to consider this during their appraisal process. In fact, any funder claiming to have green credentials will insist that applicants consider all the environmentally friendly options. Projects looking to refurbish and build a new community centre will be encouraged to look at energy-efficient heating systems, solar panels for generating hot water, environmentally friendly insulation products and the use of non-toxic paints. Tourist leaflets might be encouraged to look at using recycled paper and biodegradable inks, as well as encouraging people to explore on foot or by public transport. A child playgroup looking to establish a toy library might be encouraged to purchase wooden building blocks instead of plastic ones. Not only may these be harder wearing and longer lasting, but purchasing them from a local craftsman indirectly helps to keep that person employed, and the woodworking craft alive. Sourcing supplies from local businesses not only boosts the local economy, but it is more environmentally friendly than having goods delivered from several hundred miles away.

The impact on the local environment will also be considered. How much noise will your project make whilst it is being developed? What steps can you take to ensure that you don't upset the neighbours? Does your tourist leaflet encourage thousands of visitors to get into their cars and clog up country lanes? Would the impact be lessened if you ran the project as a minibus project showing tourists around? Could you clear scrubland in the autumn when birds and animals have finished nesting?

PROJECT MONITORING

It's all very well claiming that you are going to provide 20 volunteering opportunities, plant 75 trees, have 5,000 leaflets printed and encourage 20,000 visitors to your area, but your funder is going to want proof. Depending on how they operate, your funder may hold back some of their grant money until they have seen the proof. So it's in your interest to understand from the beginning what exactly you need to do to collect that information and evidence.

An appraiser looking at an application form where the applicant demonstrates and has enclosed examples of how their information will be collected will have greater confidence in the project. So, create the necessary forms and templates, which will help to prove how many volunteered for your project, and explain how your system of keeping track of who has each toy in your nursery group's toy library will work.

Funders are not just interested in how you will monitor your outputs though. They are also keen to know how you will monitor yourselves. It's all very well identifying when your milestone or key dates are, but whose responsibility is it to check whether they are being adhered to? What procedures do you have in place to pay invoices? Who holds the chequebook and how many signatories are needed on each cheque? An organisation that allows one signature to sign cheques, or where both signatories are related (e.g. husband and wife) could scare a funder. If they give a community group several thousand pounds, they are going to want to know that it takes more than one signature to take the money and run!

If you have a committee of members charged with implementing the project, tell your funder who they are and what their responsibilities are. Explain to your funder how often you'll meet up, how you'll resolve problems and what you'll do to keep the rest of the community group informed of your progress. Give the appraiser confidence in you, and they'll have confidence in your project.

6
The Appraisal Process

Whilst many funders ask similar questions of applicants to help them decide whether to support the project or not, the way in which they carry out that appraisal process can vary. People working for the funder will carry out an initial assessment to check that you are eligible to apply, that your community group has the legal status to apply and that your project will help promote the hopes and goals of the funding organisation.

THE BASIC PROCESS

After this initial assessment, a more thorough analysis may be undertaken where staff will examine your costs, your outputs and whether your monitoring systems are robust enough. It's at this stage that you may be contacted by a grants officer, or someone from within the organisation, to clarify points on your application form that they don't fully understand. Don't be surprised if they ask to pop out and see you; many are dying for an excuse to get out of the office!

If the funding organisation asks if they can come out and see you, try to accommodate this request. They do appreciate that not everyone from your community group or committee will be able to be there because of work or family commitments. Not only is it nice for you to be able to picture a face when you ring them in the future, but the relationship between an applicant and a funder is an important one. Anything that helps to strengthen it is to be encouraged.

Visiting an applicant helps the funder to visualise exactly what you, as a group, are hoping to achieve. Photographs are a great way of showing funders any problem areas that your project will improve, but nothing beats seeing something with your own eyes. It's also a good opportunity for the funder to ask for further information or to see a demonstration. They may even want to talk to some of the people who will benefit from your project. Be grateful for a visit, because funders can't visit every single applicant.

Depending upon the size of the grant and the funding organisation's processes, a grants officer may themselves be able to make a recommendation whether a grant should be awarded or declined. This recommendation may be examined by a supervisor or someone higher in the organisation, who will either endorse or disagree with the grant officer's recommendation.

Areas of expertise

Not all appraisers are experts at everything, but chances are, they know a man or woman who is. Your application may be sent to someone else either within the grant-funding organisation or externally for their comments. For example, if you were applying to a local authority for funding towards some playground equipment for the local private nursery, it's quite possible that someone from the council's parks and recreation department will be asked to look at your application. They will know whether the swings and slides you're hoping to purchase meet current safety guidelines, and will have a better idea as to whether your costs are realistic. Although they may not have the authority to accept or reject your application, their recommendations will be taken into consideration by the appraiser.

PARTNERSHIP PANEL APPRAISALS

An individual grant officer may make a recommendation to either approve or reject an application, but will then have to take it to a panel of members within that organisation who will then vote to make that final decision. To outsiders this can seem bureaucratic, but if the funding organisation is awarding public money, it has to demonstrate that it is administering the grant scheme responsibly. Chapter 3 explained how some councils apply to Europe or national government for funds, and how some organisations form partnerships to apply for money. The grant money they award to groups applying to them, has to meet their aims and goals, so the people who sit on these appraisal panels are responsible for ensuring that this happens. You've probably heard of the saying that 'two heads are better than one', and this process draws upon this.

When a project is discussed in a panel situation like this, it often raises questions that the initial appraiser may not even have considered. Similarly, an appraiser who has concerns over a specific project, and may be inclined to reject the application, may find that the other panel members, drawing upon their own experiences, are able to demonstrate that these fears are unfounded.

Attending panel appraisals

In the same way that an appraiser may ask to come and visit you, you might be invited to attend the appraisal panel meeting dealing with your project. Try not to let this worry you. Think of it as getting a second bite of the cherry. Not only have you been able to 'sell' your project idea on paper, you now have the opportunity to 'sell' it again, face to face. The passion of a community group can really come across at such events, and passion is a great motivator for getting things done.

An invitation to attend an appraisal panel should be scrutinised to see what will be expected of you. Are you expected to attend? For some funding organisations this meeting is a vital part of the appraisal process and without you playing your part, they will be unable to complete the appraisal process. Have a clear understanding of what is expected of you, such as:

- How many from your group are invited?
- What time will you be required and for how long?

- Are you expected to do a presentation to the panel, and if so for how long?
- What presentation equipment is available to you?

The thought of a sitting in front of a panel of people may be enough to throw some applicants into a cold sweat. It probably seems of little comfort, but try to remember that is it your project that is being appraised and judged, not your presentation skills! So what is expected of you at an appraisal panel? To make sure you are well prepared, consider the following:

- If there is anything you don't understand from the letter, contact the funding organisation and ask for clarification. If the letter doesn't say, find out who is going to be on the panel. Some organisations might not be able to give you names because they haven't been finalised at this stage – getting anything between three and ten people together at the same time can be an organisational nightmare. However, they should be able to tell you how many people will be on the panel, and which organisations they are from.

- Find out how many of your community group are expected to attend. Again, panels will understand that other commitments and time constraints make it difficult for some to attend, but remember it is a group application so try not to send just one person.

- Find out how much time you will have, what time you will be needed and how early you are allowed to turn up. The difficulties in getting lots of people together on the same day often means that appraisal panels appraise several projects at a time, so turning up ten minutes before you're due to start will mean that you won't be milling about with other applicants.

- Don't let the word 'presentation' daunt you. For many panels, what this means is that it is an opportunity for you to speak, to 'sell' your project idea without being interrupted by questions. You might find it preferable to sit in front of the panel and speak directly to them. If you have a laptop computer and can use presentation software, then create a short presentation, if you are permitted to do so. But double-check that the appraisal panel will have the necessary equipment to enable you to show your presentation. Ten people huddled around a laptop isn't particularly comfortable.

- Draw upon your community group's strengths. If someone in your group is used to giving presentations as part of their paid employment then get them to do it.

- Ensure you have all the information to hand. Whether you're doing a presentation or just chatting to the panel, make sure you have a copy of your application form with you, and take any other notes that you think you may need. This is not a school exam where you are forced to commit everything to memory. Panels would much rather you got the information right, rather than guessed.

- If your presentation time is 10 minutes, stick to 10 minutes. It's 10 minutes for a reason – the panel could have another 12 applicants to see on the same day, so a fixed time treats all applicants equally and helps the panel to keep to schedule. A 30-minute presentation does not mean that your project is three times as good as another applicant's 10-minute presentation. In fact, it suggests that you can't keep to a timescale and may make the panel question your milestones!

How panels operate will vary between funding organisations, but you should expect to be introduced to all the panel members, and told what their responsibility is on the panel. You should also be offered the chance to introduce those of your group. Someone on the appraisal panel will officially 'chair' the panel meeting, and they should explain to you how the meeting will operate. You may be asked to do your presentation or talk to start with, after which panel members may be invited by the Chair to ask you questions.

It's an appraisal – not an interrogation!

Don't be frightened by the questions. This is the panel's opportunity to try to understand your project fully. The panel members will have been given an opportunity to read your application and take on board any comments made by a grant officer or initial appraiser. Sometimes it's not always possible to get a clear understanding from the application form of exactly what the project is trying to achieve. This may not be down to how you answered the questions, but because the question wasn't asked in the first place on the application form. Answer the questions to the best of your ability, backing up your answers with any evidence that you may have brought along with you. Don't panic, if you can't answer a question. The panel can always ask that you find out the information and supply it to them as soon as possible afterwards.

Hopefully, you too will also be given an opportunity to ask any questions that you may have. Don't expect an answer to the question that everyone in your group will want to know which is, have we got the grant? Once the appraisal panel have asked all the questions they need to and answered yours, the process is over as far as you are concerned. Once you have left the room, or at a later point, the panel will consider all the information that you have provided them with, both in the application form and during the appraisal panel meeting, and will then make their decision.

All you have to do now is sit back and wait for their letter.

7

The Decision

It will feel similar to that moment all those years ago when you were waiting for your exam results to drop through the letterbox. There's a lot at stake here, not just for you, but for the community, too. Hopefully, the answer will be good news.

WHAT DOES THE OFFER LETTER MEAN?

Hooray! The letter has arrived, and good news, they want to offer you some money. Great! Go and buy some champagne and celebrate. Take time out to feel chuffed with your achievement, you deserve it!

An offer of a grant means that the funder has assessed your application and believes that your project is worthy of support. This decision has been based upon the information that you provided in your application. So, if any aspect of your project has changed, you should contact your funder immediately, because it could have implications. Your offer letter is a legally binding contract and you may have to sign a copy or a return slip and send it back to the funder to say that you agree to all of their terms and conditions.

ALWAYS READ AN OFFER LETTER CAREFULLY

Sit down somewhere quiet to read it, and then read it again. Do you understand everything that it says? Are there any guidance notes for the offer letter? If so, read them. Make a note of anything you don't understand, and if the guidance notes don't help, then contact the funder and ask questions. You must understand everything that you are being asked. Failure to do so could result in less grant money being paid out, the grant being withdrawn, or even being claimed back at a later date. Some offer letters have expiry dates. If you haven't acknowledged them or returned the signed acceptance form within the timescale, your grant may be withdrawn.

When you understand all the implications of the offer letter, sign and return the acceptance slip as soon as possible. An applicant who does this gives confidence to a funder. Just like the application form, only an authorised member of the community group should sign the offer letter or return slip. Remember the relationship that you are building up here. Send a letter with the return slip and thank the funder for their offer.

READING AND UNDERSTANDING THIS CONTRACT

An offer letter is a legally binding contract, so you must understand exactly what you are signing up to. At first sight, it may look as thick as the application form that you completed! However, whilst offer letters vary from funder to funder, there are some common points that many will include. Don't be surprised to see each point or clause in your offer letter numbered. This makes it easier for both you and your funder to refer to, should you have any queries.

- **Headings and references**. Check all the headings and references at the top of your letter. These may detail your unique project reference number which should be quoted in all correspondence, confirm the name of the funding scheme that your grant is being financed through, and provide a contact name and number for the officer within the funding organisation who will be dealing with your grant.

- **Grant amount**. After those delightful words, where the funders state how pleased they are to be able to offer you a grant, will come the important details of how much the grant is. Check this against your application form. Is it what you asked for? Is it less than you were expecting? This paragraph may also state what your total project costs can be, or refer you to an appendix, which details the type of expenditure that you can spend this grant money on. This is particularly important for projects receiving grants from more than one funder. This paragraph may also include an intervention rate, a figure expressed as a percentage, and show how much of the project's income your funder will be contributing. A funder offering a grant of £750 to a £1,000 project is offering an intervention rate of 75 per cent, because the funders' grant will cover three quarters of the total project costs. Intervention rates are explained in more detail later on pp. 109–14.

- **Application information**. You may see a clause reminding you that the offer of grant has been based upon the information in your application. If it doesn't make it explicitly clear, this is a reminder that should you need to make any changes whatsoever to your project, you need to consult with your funders before you take any action. A change to the project could change the amount or your entitlement to the grant.

- **How to accept**. Details will be given as to what you need to do to accept this grant offer. Follow these carefully, making a note of any special requests and deadlines. You could be sent two copies of the offer letter and have to sign one and return it within 30 days, or there may be a simple form bearing your project title and reference number on it, that you need to sign and return. Check to see if your funder needs you to send back any additional information. Failing to do this could result in any grant monies being held back until that information is provided. You should only accept the offer if you have the authority to do so and the conditions of grant are acceptable to your community group.

- **Claiming money, keeping records and audit requirements**. For many this is the paragraph of interest because it tells you how to get your hands on the money. It may advise on what paperwork is required, and how often the funder will need you to send a progress report of how your project is going. Such reports may only be required annually, six monthly, quarterly or only when the project is complete. There will be penalties if you fail to do this. There may be an appendix to your letter detailing the deadline dates for claims or reports. Any public body issuing public money as grant funding is also subject to external auditing from either the government's audit office, or the European audit office, if that's where the grant money comes from. Scrutinise carefully any information provided here about how long you will be expected to keep records for. Further information about this appears in Chapter 10.

- **Publicity**. Funders are not shy people. If they've awarded you some money, they may want the whole world to know about it. Here you'll find out what is expected of you, whether you'll need to include the funder's logo on your letters, project signs, press releases or any other contact that you have with the outside world.

- **Output confirmation**. Details of the outputs that your funder expects your project to meet may be listed either within the main body of your letter or as a separate appendix. Check these against those quoted in your application form. If there are any differences that you were not aware of, question your funder immediately. Signing an offer letter means that you are signing up to everything contained within it.

- **Additional requirements**. If the funding organisation you have applied to has obtained their grant money from somewhere else, then there may be rules from that funder that also apply to you. This is common for funding that comes from Europe, for example. This tends to impact more on larger, expensive projects, but it is still your responsibility to check how it applies to you and your project.

- **Complaints**. Hopefully, your application process will run smoothly, but mistakes and errors do happen from time to time. That's the problem when you allow humans to get involved with the process! As soon as any problems or difficulties arise, discuss them with your funder immediately. The sooner they are resolved the sooner you can continue with your project, which is what everyone wants in the end.

However, if for whatever reason a problem cannot be resolved, information as to who you can contact and the procedures involved should be shown here.

- **Clawback**. It sounds painful, and it could be, because it identifies occasions when funders can ask for their money back. It's rare, particularly for a community group project, but there are occasions when it could happen, and this clause will clarify those occasions. Clawback tends to happen on big capital projects involving buildings. One example would be when a business receives a grant to renovate a building to create suitable business premises, but then sells it some time after the project is complete (a successful business may need to move to larger premises earlier than anticipated). Funders often set a sliding scale, and the amount to be repaid diminishes the more time that has passed since the project's completion.

UNDERSTANDING INTERVENTION RATES

An intervention rate measures the level of financial support that a funding organisation is giving to your project. This figure is quoted as a percentage, and often appears on an offer letter followed by the phrase 'whichever is the lesser'. This means that if your project costs less than anticipated, they will not pay out the full grant figure that they are offering. However, by offering a percentage, the total cost of the project is still covered. It is important that you understand this because it affects how your project is funded should any of the costs change.

Imagine your project is anticipated to cost £1,200, and your funder has agreed to award you a grant of £900 or 75 per cent, whichever is the lesser. What does this mean, and what impact does the phrase 'whichever is the lesser' have?

1. If your project costs are exactly £1,200, then 75 per cent of this figure is £900, which is the same as the amount of grant they have offered. You can claim £900. The £900 figure and the 75 per cent figure are exactly the same. There is no 'lesser' amount.

2. If your project costs are lower, say £1,100, then 75 per cent of £1,100 is £825. You can claim £825 because this intervention rate is the 'lesser' amount – it is less than the £900 grant figure offered. The project hasn't cost as much, so you don't need as much grant money.

3. If your project costs are higher, say £1,300, then 75 per cent of £1,300 is £975. You can claim £900 because this is the 'lesser' amount – it is less that the figure generated by the intervention rate of 75 per cent.

The 'whichever is the lesser' phrase helps funders to keep control over their contributions. If they offered you a fixed amount of grant money and your project cost less, then you could end up making a profit! If they just offered a percentage, and your costs increased drastically, the funding organisation would end up paying out more money than it had anticipated.

For some community group projects, where only one funding organisation is involved, the intervention rate is easy to understand and follow. Imagine you have a project which will cost £1,200 in total. It might be funded as follows:

Table 12. Funders and their intervention rates

Funder	Amount	Intervention rate
Applicant (your group)	£300	25%
Funding organisation	£900	75%
Totals	**£1,200**	**100%**

You can see here that the organisation that is giving you the money to achieve your project is providing 75 per cent of the funding. Essentially, this means that when you pay an invoice relating to your project, 25 per cent will come from your own money, and the grant money will pay the other 75 per cent.

Intervention rates can seem complicated when there is more than one organisation providing grant money. The intervention rates, or the percentages, may look strange, but the principle remains the same. Let's imagine that our £1,200 project is actually funded as follows:

Table 13. Intervention rates on a project funded by several organisations

Funder	Amount	Intervention rate
Applicant (your group)	£100	8.35%
Parish council	£270	22.49%
Local council	£230	19.16%
Lottery funding	£600	50%
Totals	**£1,200**	**100%**

At first glance, some of those intervention rates look horrendous. Wouldn't life be so much simpler if we didn't have to deal with decimals? Don't let the decimals scare you. Just remember that the percentage figure explains how much of the total project each funder is paying for, so, therefore, how much of each invoice each funder is effectively paying for. Imagine that your project now receives an invoice for £500. Based on the intervention rates, this is how much each funder will be contributing to that invoice:

Table 14. Proportion of invoice paid as per intervention rate

Funder	Intervention rate	Amount
Applicant	8.35%	£41.75
Parish council	22.49%	£112.45
Local council	19.16%	£95.80
Lottery funding	50%	£250.00
Totals	**100%**	**£500.00**

So you will be paying £41.75 from your own group funds, because that's 8.35 per cent of the £500 invoice. The parish council will be paying £112.45, because that's 22.49 per cent, the local council £95.80 and so on.

But if you know that your project will cost £1,200 and all of your funders are going to contribute a total of £1,200, why bother with intervention rates at all? Well, percentages help to keep the system fair. The costs that you end up paying may differ from those on your application form. A walk around your local supermarket will show you how quickly some prices change. Technological or computer equipment prices can drop drastically as new technology arrives on the scene. The costs that you have identified on your application form are not cast-iron guaranteed prices.

Let's imagine that the £500 invoice we used in the example above actually comes in cheaper, at £400. If there were no intervention rates, how would you decide which funder should help to pay for it? Is it fair to ask the lottery funding to pay for it all, and none of the other funders? There will be more invoices to pay over the lifetime of the project, but at the end, your total project costs may come in at £1,100, and not the £1,200 as suggested on your application form. So who should benefit from that £100 saving? Do you reduce the contribution from the lottery funding by £100 because they are contributing the most? Do you reduce the amount from one of the other funders instead? If so, which one? Whatever you do, without intervention rates, you will upset someone.

Equality

Try to think of this from the funder's point of view, too. Remember, when they appraised your project, they were also considering the value for money. They considered the outputs they were getting, compared against the amount of grant money they were giving to you. Well, if you've saved £100, and you give that £100 saving to one funder, that means that that particular funder is now getting better value for money if you manage to achieve the same outputs. But because you passed the whole saving to just one funder, all the other funders are missing the opportunity of getting better value for money.

Intervention rates do away with this inequality. If the project makes savings, then *all* of the funders benefit. And those savings help all of those funders offer more money to more groups. You, as the applicant, also benefit from those savings, because your contribution will reduce proportionately, too.

Of course, prices don't just fall, they go up as well. Not only that, but your project may encounter costs that no one has considered. Intervention rates help in this situation, too. If your project costs rise, you can't assume that your funders will automatically cover that cost. They too have limited cash!

AS SOON AS YOU NOTICE THAT YOUR COSTS ARE INCREASING, OR YOU HIT A PROBLEM, SPEAK TO YOUR FUNDERS IMMEDIATELY

Some funding organisations may be happy to accommodate a 10 per cent increase in costs and their associated grant. Funders live in the same world as you. They know that inflation exists out there and unexpected costs arise. Even if your funder offers this margin, it is still imperative that you liaise with them and keep them informed.

If your costs have risen, you may find that all of your funders are able to help out, and their intervention rates may remain the same. Let's imagine that your project costs have increased from £1,200 to £1,500. If all the funders were able to help proportionately, the intervention rates would remain the same, but the maximum grant figures would now be greater.

Table 15. Change in total grant awarded

Funder	Previous amount	Previous intervention rate	New amount	New intervention rate
Applicant (your group)	£100	8.35%	£125.25	8.35%
Parish council	£270	22.49%	£337.35	22.49%
Local council	£230	19.16%	£287.40	19.16%
Lottery funding	£600	50%	£750.00	50%
Totals	**£1,200**	**100%**	**£1,500.00**	**100%**

However, if you have several funders, not all of them will be willing (or able) to offer more cash. As a result, one funder may come to the rescue, which will alter all the intervention rates for all of the other funders, too. Let's look at what happens to the intervention rates when the local council agrees to fund the £300 increase.

Table 16. Change in intervention rates

Funder	Previous amount	Previous intervention rate	New amount	New intervention rate
Applicant (your group)	£100	8.35%	£100	6.66%
Parish council	£270	22.49%	£270	18%
Local council	£230	19.16%	£530	35.34%
Lottery funding	£600	50%	£600	40%
Totals	**£1,200**	**100%**	**£1,500**	**100%**

Although the only funder to increase their offer is the local council, this has had an impact on the intervention rates of all of the funders. The local council's intervention rate has increased, whilst all the others have reduced.

Whenever a funder amends the amount of grant they are providing, or the intervention rate of their grant, you will receive confirmation in writing. This could be in the form of a letter, or you may receive a brand-new offer letter, which you'll need to formally sign and accept.

Intervention rates may seem complicated, but in reality, they help keep equality and fairness to all parties involved in your project.

REJECTION – WHAT LESSONS CAN BE LEARNED?

What happens though if the letter you get isn't good news? Rejection is hard to take, but please remember that they are not rejecting you personally. There are numerous reasons why your project might be rejected, some of which will be entirely beyond your control. The letter you receive should give you the reasons why. If there is anything that you don't understand, contact the funder and ask them to explain.

Ineligibility

Checking whether your group or your project is eligible to apply is one of the first steps you should take before you even complete an application form. Yet groups still apply to inappropriate funders, and they will be rejected because of it. It is a waste of everyone's time, and can become demoralising. If this happens to you, learn from your mistake and read the eligibility criteria of all future funders before you begin completing their application forms.

Project already started

Many funders will not support a project that has already begun, so if they've discovered that your project has started, they could reject you on these grounds. One of the main reasons that groups apply for grant funding is because they can't afford the project themselves. Starting a project before you've received an offer letter means that you are risking the limited resources that your community group has. As the previous chapters have illustrated, an appraisal of your application form is not just an examination of the financial need of your project, but also an assessment of whether your project resolves the problems or issues it is trying to address, and whether you are the best people to do this. If you've applied to several funders for money, and they all come back and say that your project doesn't solve the problem, any money that you've already spent has been wasted.

Funders won't consider retrospective applications. If you've been able to pay for the project in the first place then you've actually demonstrated that there isn't any need for the grant money!

GRANT FUNDING SHOULD PROVIDE
ADDITIONALITY

This means that the grant money itself makes the difference of whether a project will go ahead or not, or that the grant money will allow the project to achieve more. In other words, the grant money helps to increase the amount of benefit to come out of your project. If it doesn't, then the grant money is being wasted, and no funder can afford or be seen to be wasting money.

Starting a project because you are sure that you will get the funding is arrogant and won't be tolerated. If all the funder's guidance notes clearly state that your project must not start until you have received an offer or permission-to-start notice from them in writing and you still go ahead, it suggests that you cannot follow guidelines and procedures. If you can't follow those, how can the funder be sure that you'll even complete the project?

Of course, there are always exceptions, and one relates to building works. If you've applied for funding which includes the renovation of a building, and you have to carry out emergency structural works to prevent the building from collapsing, then you may be allowed to carry out some of the strengthening work that you were going to do as part of your project.

YOU MUST ALWAYS SPEAK TO YOUR FUNDER FIRST BEFORE DOING ANY WORK

Always get any such permission from them in writing, before carrying out any work.

Not enough money

Funding organisations never have enough money to go around. You might have a great project, but if the funder doesn't have sufficient money, they can't help you out even though they would love to. There is little you can do here, apart from begin looking for another funder. Remember to keep this rejection letter though, to show to your next funder as evidence of who you have already approached.

APPEALING AGAINST THE DECISION

It is difficult not to feel aggrieved when you discover that your application has been declined. For some groups, it will have taken guts and determination to get as far as submitting an application. Your immediate reaction might be to fight on and appeal in some way. Don't.

Firstly, for those funding organisations whose money comes from private sources, remember, it is their money to do with as they wish. You don't have a right to their money.

Secondly, when an application is declined, it is because of a specific reason. If you are ineligible, then you are ineligible! You don't meet the criteria, move on and find a funder whose criteria you do meet. If the funder has no more money available, appealing against the decision won't create any more money for the funder to give you.

If you feel that you have new information to support your application, then speak to the funder and find out what options are available to you. You may be advised to submit a new application with this extra information. Completing a new application form will be relatively straightforward because you now have experience of answering the questions that the funder has asked.

If the only person you've been dealing with is someone from the funding organisation, ask them if they can give you any constructive feedback on your application. Is there anything that you could do better or differently next time?

Making an appeal suggests that you don't have confidence in the funding organisation's decision-making process. If that is the case, then ask yourself, what sort of applicant-funder relationship are you creating by appealing?

The Bevelshire Partnership

BEVELSHIRE PARTNERSHIP

**The Bevelshire Partnership, Bevelshire House, Beveltown,
Bevelshire BV1 1TN**

Mr R. Weed
Bevel Gate Gardening Club
c/o The Grass Cuttings
Bevel Gate
Bevelshire
BV12 1VB

Tel: 01657 882937

Email: ppartners@
Bevelshirepartnership.gov.uk

30 November 20XX

Dear Mr Weed

ENVIRONMENTAL GRANT SCHEME

Project Title: Bevel Gate Community Garden Project

Project Ref: HL/BGComGar

I am pleased to inform you that the Bevelshire Partnership has approved your application for grant funding for the above project. The amount of grant that we are offering is **£6,150** or **67.95 per cent whichever is the lesser**, based upon your total project costs of £9,050.

If you wish to accept this grant offer, please read the terms and conditions listed below in full and then sign, date the copy letter enclosed and return it to me within 30 days. **Please read the terms and conditions carefully as they form the contract and responsibilities to which you are committing your group.** Please do not hesitate to contact me if you are unsure of any of the conditions.

Fig. 4. Bevel Gate Gardening Club offer letter.

1. The eligible start date for this project is the **1 January (20YY). Any expenditure incurred before this date is ineligible for grant support**.

2. The grant is subject to the money being made available by the partners of the Bevelshire Partnership (Bevelshire County Council, Bevelshire Environmental Trust and the Regional Development Agency).

3. The first 75 per cent of grant money will be released upon receipt of a signed acceptance of this offer. The remaining 25 per cent will be released upon receipt of a satisfactory end-of-project monitoring form. Grant monies may be withheld if this monitoring form does not meet the satisfaction of Bevelshire Partnership staff. The final instalment of grant money will be released using the intervention rate details above, and only upon evidence of all defrayed expenditure. Failure to submit claims may lead your grant being withdrawn.

4. You will be expected to report on your achievement to date on the outputs identified in Appendix 1. Any confusion about the outputs identified here should be clarified immediately.

5. You can only claim grant funding towards costs that fall into the expenditure categories detailed in Appendix 2.

6. Your milestones are included in Appendix 3.

7. End-of-project monitoring forms should be returned within 30 days of the end of the project. Failure to return them within this timescale may lead to your grant being withdrawn.

8. Once your final monitoring report has been submitted, the Bevelshire Partnership may ask for the evidence of your expenditure to be audited by a qualified auditor. We may retain up to 5 per cent of your final payment until this auditing procedure has been carried out to our satisfaction.

9. You must notify us of any changes that occur to your project. This grant has been awarded solely on the information provided by you prior to our appraisal.

10. All projects funded by the partnership must publicise their support. Use of the partnership's logo should take place on all publicity material that you produce. An electronic copy of our logos can be provided upon request.

▶

11. You are required to offer the partnership an invitation to any publicity event that you arrange, although we are under no obligation to attend every event.

12. Copies of any publicity material, press releases or adverts are to be included with the relevant quarterly report.

13. You must ensure that you have sufficient systems in place to monitor project expenditure and outputs achieved. Any evidence of impropriety may lead to the grant offer being withdrawn.

14. You must adhere to current law at all times, including any legislation brought in during the operation of your project.

15. The sale of any assets purchased using grant money from the partnership can only take place with the agreement of the partnership. The partnership may expect a contribution from the sale of the asset, as a reimbursement of grant payment towards that particular asset.

Yours sincerely

Peter Partners

Environmental Grant Scheme Coordinator

Appendix 1 – Outputs

Quantity	Output
2	New community facility created
629	Additional people using new facility
25	Directly involved volunteers
190	Number of people given access to new learning opportunities
1750sqm	Area of land enhanced

Appendix 2 – Expenditure categories

Expenditure item	Expenditure category	Total projected spend
Hire of rotavator, skip and earth mover for two days (in-kind)	Equipment hire	£500
Topsoil removal and disposal, replacement topsoil	Land improvements	£2,300
Installation of electricity and water	Utilities	£2,500
Plants and seeds	Equipment	£500
Seats, benches and paving	Equipment	£500
Shed, communal community garden equipment	Equipment	£650
Boundary fence, gate	Security fixtures	£1,200
Volunteer time (in-kind)	Volunteer	£900
Total		**£9,050**

Appendix 3 – Milestones

Milestone	Target
1st weekend in January 20YY	Volunteers clear excess undergrowth from site.
2nd weekend in January 20YY	Site cleared using hire equipment, old topsoil removed.
3rd week in January 20YY	Electricity and water companies install services.
3rd weekend in January 20YY	Replacement top soil delivered. Volunteers begin creating community garden infrastructure – raised beds, wildlife pond and pathways. Boundary fencing erected around community garden perimeter.
4th weekend in January 20YY	Gardening Club storage shed erected.
1st weekend in February 20YY	Complete hard landscaping.
3rd weekend in February 20YY	Communal garden equipment purchased.
4th weekend in February 20YY	Wildlife garden planting completed.

Appendix 4 – Profiled monitoring reports

Form issued	Covering period	Deadline for return
7 April 20YY	1 January 20YY to 31 March 20YY	30 April 20YY

8
Project Implementation

You've been offered the money, you've sent back all of the forms, and now the exciting work begins. It's time to get cracking on your project, and delivering what you said you would in your application form. Does everyone in your community group know what they are doing and when they need to do it by?

MONITORING YOUR PROJECT

Use the key dates or milestones that you laid out in your application form as a means of keeping a check on your project to see if it is running to schedule. This is why funders ask you for milestones, because planning ahead helps you focus on which actions take priority at each stage of the project. If you produced a business or action plan at the start to help you determine what those key dates were, use it now to help you achieve your goals.

Communication

If you have established a project development group as suggested in Chapter 1, then it should be meeting regularly. Some funders like to see a project management structure, which details the names of people who can sign documents, those who will coordinate each aspect of the project and how often you'll get together to share information.

Sharing information is vital if there are several members of the community group involved. Try to avoid ringing other members by phone. Not only does it run the risk of missing somebody out if they happen to be out, but it runs the risk that not everybody will be told exactly the same information. That is where confusion can arise.

Face-to-face meetings help to avoid this, so arrange to meet regularly to start with. As your project develops and everyone becomes clear about what their role is, it may not be necessary to meet up as often. Conversely, if you encounter a problem, consider meeting more frequently until the problem is resolved.

Don't forget to keep the rest of the community group informed of how your project is progressing. Share the good news as well as the bad news, and accept help from other members to overcome difficulties. Remember that your priority is to get the project completed, not save face.

Delegate

Remember, a community group project is the responsibility of the whole group, not just a few. If the workload is getting too much for those in the project development group, get more members involved. Break down jobs into smaller, manageable chunks. Instead of asking one person to buy the toys, books and play equipment for your nursery project, get one person to buy toys, one to buy books and another to buy the play equipment. It's easier for people to find small amounts of time to tackle smaller jobs than it is for people to find large chunks of time to tackle big jobs. The easier a task is to achieve, the quicker people will do it. People put off difficulties, and that's where delays can creep in.

Keep a diary

Not just for recording appointments with suppliers and other key dates, but for recording details of events that happen whilst you're delivering your project. Keep a note of what went well or of any difficulties that you experienced. This will help you when it's time to complete a monitoring report for your funders.

Keep taking pictures

Don't just think of pictures for your 'before' and 'after' shots, take them as you go about implementing your project. Including images with your interim monitoring reports clearly demonstrates to funders the progress you have achieved to date. Exercise caution when taking pictures of projects that include children, particularly if you want to use them for publicity purposes. Always obtain permission from the adult responsible. At the end of the project, you might want to take some 'cheesy' pictures of any officials cutting ribbons, unveiling plaques or making speeches. Funders and the local press love them, even if you hate being in them!

MEASURING YOUR RESULTS

As soon as you begin to implement your project, if not before, you should be recording information that verifies your outputs. Think about the systems that you need to have in place which will allow you to give your funders all the evidence that they will need to verify your achievements.

Invoices and receipts

When a funder reviews your project, either at its completion or while it is still in progress, they will want to see the evidence of the money you are spending. This means keeping *all* invoices and receipts. Keep these project-related paper records separate from your normal day-to-day invoices and receipts. Set up a file specifically for project expenditure and give each invoice a reference number. A referencing system doesn't have to be complicated, a simple table or spreadsheet that you maintain as each invoice or payment is processed will make completing your claim and monitoring forms much easier.

Table 17. Example financial recording system

Ref. no	Amount	Supplier	Description	Expenditure category	Date paid	Chq no
001	£49.99	Hardware shop	Tools	Equipment hire	14/11/XX	100239
002	£179.82	Hire shop	Sanding equipment	Equipment hire	22/11/XX	100248
003	£2.99	Stationers	Pens	Stationery	23/11/XX	Petty cash

Numbering each invoice or receipt in ascending order means that it's easy to check that you've collected them all before sending them off to your funder. Recording the cheque number against each payment also helps your funders double-check them against your bank statements, particularly if you have two cheques for the same amount.

If you've been awarded grants from several funders, some of whom have only awarded the grant against certain types of expenditure, you could include a column in your table to help you identify which expenditure category receipts and invoices relate to. Again, the reference number allocated will help you to locate them quickly when the time comes to provide that specific funder with all the information.

Legal documentation

Are there any legal documents required at different stages of your project? Projects that involve building works of some kind may need planning approvals or regular inspections to ensure that building works are safe and meet current guidelines. Keep any certificates or legal notices in date order to make them easier to find, and make a note if any are required to be seen by your funders. Some may not release all of the grant money until they've seen copies. If your project requires planning permission and you've not obtained it, funding organisations will not want to be seen supporting groups that don't obey the law of the land.

Proving outputs

Some outputs are easy to prove. If one of your outputs is the creation of a new community centre, then that whacking great big building on the plot of land where there wasn't one before (because you've got pictures to prove it) will be evidence in itself. Don't forget that funders can come and see it for themselves if they happen to be in the area. If they are local to you, they may decide to drive home the scenic route one night!

Invoices will also help to prove outputs. If you've stated that you're going to plant 300 tree saplings, then the funding organisation will expect to see an invoice for 300 tree saplings somewhere in your report. They will then check your bank statements to ensure that a payment of the same amount has left your account.

So, with physical assets, proving the outputs is relatively straightforward. Funding organisations can come and inspect them with their own eyes if they so wish (another excuse for getting out of the office) as well as tie them up to the existing paperwork that you have supplied to them. But what about outputs which aren't physical?

A typical example is one mentioned earlier concerning volunteering opportunities, which might also form part of your monetary claim, if you're using it as in-kind support. You need to prove the volunteer existed, and how long they helped you out. This is easy with a simple form.

Table 18. Example volunteer sheet

PROJECT NAME				
Volunteer name:				
Volunteer address:				
Date	Description of activities	Start time	End time	No. of hours
Volunteer signature..				

Having a form like this helps you out in several ways. One form for each volunteer means that you can easily prove how many volunteers have helped throughout the project. The fact that you've collected their names and addresses means that the funder can carry out a spot check and contact that person to verify this information. Getting volunteers to sign the sheet makes them take responsibility. If they sign and they haven't done the work then that is fraud, particularly if it's helped your community group claim funds. The form also helps you to keep track of the total number of hours volunteered.

You should also remember that forms such as these help to corroborate other information that you give in a report to your funders. Imagine that one of your key milestone dates was to clear some land by 30 September. If it didn't happen until a week later, don't lie on your report form and say that it did happen on 30 September when you've got twenty signed volunteer sheets, all stating that these volunteers cleared scrubland on 7 October! Funders look at the whole picture.

But what if your project is to have a fun day, or a festival at your local park, and one of the outputs is that 200 local people will attend? How do you prove that? Funders can't expect them all to give you their name and addresses and sign to say that they turned up, can they? No. That would be impractical. So think of how else you can record this number. Will you be charging a small entry fee? If so, the amount of money collected will help demonstrate numbers. If you receive £200 in entry fees and charge £1 per person to enter, it demonstrates that 200 people turned up. Alternatively, if your festival or fun day is free to enter, hand out a numbered ticket to everyone who passes through your entrance, which can be used to enter a raffle to win a prize. The number of tickets issued demonstrates the number of people at your event.

Whatever your outputs may be, always discuss them with your funders and find out from them what evidence they want to see. You won't be the only project to have to prove this particular set of outputs. Other projects will have done this beforehand. Funding organisations can give you plenty of advice about what they need to see, the important point is that whatever system you have in place to record the information, you must have it ready for when you need it. It's no good having 50 volunteers turn up one day to help with your project, if you have no system in place to record and prove this fact. Proving a fact at a later date can be very difficult indeed.

COMPLETING REPORT FORMS

Filling out an application form for a grant explains to funding organisations why you need the money and how you are going to spend it. Once they've given you the money, the funders will then want to know what you've done with it, and what happened as a result. That's a cue for another form to arrive on the scene.

Monitoring reports may be required at various stages of your project, much of it depending upon the size of your project, the size of your grant and the time it takes to implement this. A project that simply buys some planters and plants to put in them, improving the visual environment of an area, may be completed within a matter of weeks. Whereas a project that sees the refurbishment of a community centre, or the provision of a training course, may take months before it is finished.

Projects that receive relatively small amounts of funding and are quick to implement, may only have one report to complete at the end. Projects which run over several months and are awarded larger grants may find themselves completing one or more interim reports and then a final report at the completion stage.

This regular reporting system may seem like bureaucracy gone mad. Let's face it; if you didn't have to spend all the time completing reports, you might stand a chance of actually getting your project finished! Yet the report is an important monitoring and communication tool. It helps funders to account to their board of trustees, or their own funders, on how their money is being spent. More importantly, it gives many funders the information they require to enable them to release a payment to you.

A monitoring form also gives funders the information they need to keep track of how a project is progressing and allows them to pick up on any problems so they can offer help and advice. Treat a monitoring report with the same respect that you gave the application form. Whereas an application form helped you to win the money, a monitoring report may mean the difference between the next instalment of money being released or held back. So what sort of information is required in a monitoring form?

Contact details

These vary from funder to funder. You might be required to complete full name and address contact details, or alternatively, your project name may be all that is required. Always quote any grant reference number that your funder has given you.

Project update

You will then be required to give an update on how your project is progressing. Are you meeting your key dates or milestones? Did the project start when you said it would? Will it or did it finish when you anticipated it would? Don't worry about questions that ask you whether anything has gone wrong. Complete them honestly. It's quite feasible that a complication may arise that neither you nor your funders considered. Whenever any complications arise, always discuss them with your funders immediately. However, even though you may have solved the problem and moved on from it, you should still refer to it in your monitoring forms. Tell your funders how you overcame the difficulty. They may use this to give advice to other projects in the future. On the other hand, has something gone well? Pass on the good news, particularly if it is something that your funder has helped you with.

Outputs

If you are completing an interim report, declare any outputs that you've achieved so far, and include the proof. It may be that, at this stage of your project, no outputs will have been achieved. Don't worry about this. Funders will see from your application form and milestones at what stage you should start achieving your outputs. If you've nothing to report, then state this clearly in the space provided. Never leave a question unanswered.

For a final report, include all the evidence needed to prove the outputs that you have achieved. Again, be honest. If you said that you would provide 12 training places, and you only provided 10, state this and then explain why. Not every project achieves and meets every single one of its target outputs. There are many external factors that can influence this. But funders expect you to make an effort to try, so detail the actions you took to meet your targets.

If you achieve over and above what you thought you would, great! Include the actual figures. If your application form said you would offer 12 training places, and you actually achieved 15, then put 15 down on your form. Don't think that your funder is expecting 12, so that's the figure you should enter. Be honest at all times.

It's quite possible that whilst you were running your project you realised that another output could be achieved, without the need for additional funds. Include it in your report and be proud of it.

Outcomes

You may remember from Chapter 4 that as well as the measurable outputs, your project may have other outcomes, which aren't quite as easy to measure or quantify. For some projects, the impact of these outcomes won't be seen until some time after its completion. As a result, funders may make a note to contact you again in the future, long after the final grant payment has been made. This may be a condition in your offer letter and therefore part of the contract that you signed up to.

Statement of income and expenditure

Whether you are completing an interim or a final report, funders will want to know how much you have spent so far, or in total, and whether you spent within the budgets you'd identified in your application form. They may ask for a statement of income and expenditure, which is a list of the total amount of money you received for your project, broken down by funder, and the total expenditure incurred, broken down into expense categories.

Alternatively, the monitoring form may have a section to collect this information, comprising three columns: the budget heading, the budget (the figure you suggested in your application form) and then the actual figure.

Table 19. Example budgetary section of monitoring form

Budget heading	Budgeted expenditure	Actual expenditure
Publicity material	£2,000	£2,129.32
Distribution	£500	£149.99
Advertising	£1,500	£1,470

There may also be a similar breakdown required for the funding (the income) element to your project. Again, be honest and clear. Claiming grant money is explained further in the next chapter, but your funders will be able to double-check your figures based upon the information that you give them. Make sure that all of your figures add up, and if this is the final report, check that your total project income from all of your funders, based upon the intervention rates quoted in their offer letters, will cover the total project expenditure. If your project costs less than you forecast, the intervention rates should mean that your funder's contributions will be reduced proportionately, and you won't make a profit. If your project costs are higher than you budgeted, you will either have to make up the shortfall yourself, or liaise with your funders to see if they can help you out. However, if you've been monitoring your project tightly, and remained in close contact with your funders, you should not suddenly discover an overspend at this late stage.

If you are completing an interim report, your funder may ask you to estimate how much of their grant money you may need over the next three to six months. By adding up the figures from all the monitoring reports returned to them, they will then calculate how much money they need as an organisation in the immediate future. Private trusts who have their money invested may need to give notice to withdraw cash from certain investment products, for example. Grant schemes operated by local authorities or organisations who themselves are funded by national government or Europe will also need to tell their funders how much money they are likely to need over the coming months.

Some funders ask to see a certified statement of income and expenditure for a project when it is finished. This means that the statement has been signed by the relevant person within your community group. If you are a small group, this will probably be your Treasurer. However, for larger groups or those with charitable status, this may mean asking your accountant to sign it. If you are unclear, check with your funder.

Return dates

Always return the monitoring form by the deadline date provided by your funder. Failure to do so could result in a delay in processing your grant payment. Remember that some funding organisations are in exactly the same position as you. If they had to apply to Europe or national government for their funding, they too will have a monitoring form to complete and a deadline to meet. In order to meet their deadline, they have to impose deadlines upon you. Help them to help you.

PUBLICITY AND LOGOS

Not only do funders give you money, they want the whole world to know about it. Many funders issue press releases announcing to national and local press the projects that their money is helping to support. They want the public to know that these projects may not have happened if it wasn't for their money. It also helps to attract future applications, too.

Your offer letter will state when and where you will be expected to use the logo of your funding organisations. They will provide copies of the logo digitally so that you can include it on any press releases that you send out, or on newsletters, and any publicity material. If your project involves the employment of a worker, you may be expected to include their logo on the job advert that you place. If you are renovating your local community centre, your funders may expect you to erect an information board that explains to passers-by what work is going on and who is funding it.

Whenever you next walk by a historic building with scaffolding, stop and take a look. Can you see an information panel? Does it say what work is taking place and when it hopes to be completed by? Then have a look at the logos on it. Many will represent a funding organisation.

What about the funding organisations that you have applied to for your money? If your local council has received money from Europe to run a grant scheme, you may well have seen the European logo on the information leaflet telling you all about the grant. This will have been a requirement of the grant, as set out in the offer letter from Europe to your local authority. If the council has added some of their own money to the European money, they will insist that you use the European logo and their logo, because the grant scheme you have applied to is funded by both organisations.

Fig. 5. Bevelshire Partnership logo.

Generally, the funders will want you to use their logo whenever your activities come into contact with the public, but if you're unsure, contact them to find out.

Whenever you do use their logos on publicity material, try to keep a copy. For example, if you used the logo in a job advert you placed in the paper, then take a photocopy when it appears. If you're producing tourist information leaflets, funders will expect the logo to appear on them, so keep some back. Take a picture of the information board outside your community centre. Keep copies of any articles that appear in your local press. When the time comes to submit a monitoring report, enclose this material that demonstrates that you have used their logos. It proves that you are meeting their requests as laid down in their offer letter to you.

BEVEL GATE GARDENING CLUB'S SYSTEMS

The Chairman, Secretary, Treasurer and four other volunteers from the Gardening Club have formed a project committee, to oversee the day-to-day implementation of the project. They all live in the village, so have agreed to meet weekly at the Chairman's house to bring each other up to date. In the event of any problems occurring between meetings, the Chairman will be contacted. The Secretary agrees to bring the rest of the Gardening Club up to date with the project at its normal monthly meetings.

The Treasurer has made it clear that all invoices are to be addressed to the Gardening Club but sent care of his address. He will keep a record of each invoice, the expenditure category it falls into and details of the cheque number used to pay it. One of the volunteers has agreed to take pictures every day as she walks past the site on her way to work, to create a photographic record of the changes, whilst the Secretary has agreed to keep a diary.

One committee volunteer agrees to look after the other volunteers and the required record-keeping for their in-kind support.

They've created standard forms and it will be their responsibility to ensure that all forms are correctly completed, signed and dated so that they can be used as evidence for the projects grant claim. A second volunteer agrees to be responsible for arranging refreshments for the volunteers who come and help clear the land.

A third volunteer from the project committee, who lives next door to the wasteland, agrees to be the point of contact for the utility services when they come to install the water and electricity supplies, and has a key to enable the utility companies to access the site. A fourth volunteer offers to help with publicity to promote the new facility.

Once the project is physically complete, the Secretary and Treasurer will get together to complete the monitoring form, but the project committee will then meet in full to review this and to ensure that all the evidence is attached to the claim.

9
Claiming Your Grant Money

It may seem strange that the chapter about claming your grant money appears so late in the book. Surely funders dish out the grant money as soon as you've signed and returned the offer letter, don't they? How else are you supposed to pay for everything? That's the whole reason for needing a grant in the first place, isn't it?

Actually, some funders don't pay up straight away. Some may send you a cheque for the full amount at this stage, others may release a proportion of your grant, and some won't release a penny. Details of the claiming procedures will be explained in their offer letter to you. If you signed and returned the offer letter, then you have signed up to their claims procedure. Some funders will expect you to order your equipment or services first, pay the invoices and then claim the money back from them.

Your eyes are probably filling with horror as you read this, and wondering what was the point of going to all that effort to obtain a grant in the first place, if you have to have the money to be able to pay for everything before claiming it back. Understanding the claims procedure is therefore vital.

HOW TO CLAIM

Follow the advice given in your offer letter. If you don't understand it, speak with the funder before you sign and return it. Remember, it's a legal contract that you are signing up to. Essentially, a claim for grant means providing all the evidence of your expenditure. So, how do claiming procedures vary?

The upfront payment

This is probably what you originally expected from a grant-funding organisation, and some funders will do this, particularly with relatively small grants. Once you have signed the offer letter and returned it to your funders, the cheque will arrive in the post. You will still have to complete a final report, detailing your expenditure and showing how you spent the money, but if you don't spend all of the grant money, you may be expected to repay what you haven't used. The upfront payment does mean that if you haven't complied with the conditions of your grant, you might have to repay some or all of it.

Instalments

Some funders feel that they are taking a risk if they release all of their grant money upfront. Not every project goes according to plan, and if they've already given the money to a project that has spent it all, a funder may have little opportunity to claim it back. The solution is to release the money in instalments. The percentage of those instalments will vary from funder to funder, but it could work as follows:

Table 20. Grant payments released in instalments

Instalment	Percentage of frant	Paid
First	50%	Upon return of signed offer letter.
Second	35%	Upon return of satisfactory interim report.
Third	15%	Upon return of satisfactory final report.

By issuing the bulk of grant upon receipt of the signed offer letter, the funder knows that you will be able to get on with your project. Delivering the grant across several instalments helps the community group's cash flow. Projects that are funded by more than one organisation, will also be receiving grant money in accordance with those funder's offer letters and, as mentioned earlier, many community groups will be expected to make a contribution themselves from their own resources.

Releasing further instalments upon receipt of an interim monitoring form is a way of ensuring that you actually complete the form and send it in! Funders need that information for their own monitoring purposes, so linking it to a grant payment is a great carrot to dangle in front of you from a stick. The same goes for withholding some of the grant until the final report has been sent in. Not only does this give you the incentive to send it in, but it also allows the funder to review the project and adjust the level of grant paid, should the project under spend.

Satisfaction

Note the word 'satisfactory' in Table 19. If the funder isn't happy with the progress a project is making, they could withhold the next grant payment until progress is made. Whilst this may seem draconian, it can also be argued that if the project isn't as far advanced as it should be, it won't have the need for the next payment at this stage. It's yet another incentive to encourage a project to try to adhere to its own key dates and milestones. Don't feel that these are get-out clauses for the funders to withhold payment just for the sheer fun of it. It's just as important to them that projects claim all the grant money they are entitled to, and deliver the projects as promised. Projects will only be 'penalised' in this way if they fail to deliver what they promise, and that failure is a result of their own actions. You shouldn't be penalised for delays that are caused by external sources which are outside of your control.

Quarterly returns

Some grant schemes require a quarterly monitoring form giving the funder an update on the achievements made during the last three months. These quarterly returns may also be the mechanism to claim the grant payment towards the project's expenditure over the past three months. This system tends to operate for larger projects that receive larger grants. It benefits the funding organisation because it means that they are only releasing their grant money against actual expenditure that the project has incurred and paid for. From the community group's point of view, it means that you can expect a regular drip-feeding of grant money on a quarterly basis. However, it can cause some projects, particularly those run by smaller community groups, cash-flow problems.

Many small community groups apply for funding because they don't have the resources to pay for a one-off project. Whilst this quarterly reporting and claiming system still means that they don't have to pay for the whole project first before they can claim any money, it does mean that they need to have enough money to begin with to pay for the first three months' worth of invoices. If the project is large enough, three months' invoices may still be larger than the limited resources that the group has available. What happens then? The only advice that can be given is to talk to your funder. Explain the situation and enquire whether they are willing to give you some of your grant money in advance. This may be referred to as 'up-front funding' or 'bankrolling'.

Bankrolling

A funder may look at your project and, after consulting with you, decide on how much they think you will spend in the first three months. If they agree to bankroll, they may give you that amount of grant money at the beginning of the quarterly period. Then when the time comes for you to complete the claim form, the actual expenditure will be known. If you've spent more, they'll release that additional grant money as they normally would after the grant claim, along with the next instalment of advance grant monies. If you've spent less, they may reduce the next quarterly advance payment accordingly.

Let's imagine that a project has been awarded a grant of £20,000 to run a crèche facility for local parents who need a couple of hours to themselves to study and gain new qualifications. The project anticipates spending £5,000 per quarter, but only has £1,500 in its own bank accounts. It asks its funder to consider bankrolling, and the funder agrees at the rate of £5,000 per quarter. The claims and payments could work as follows:

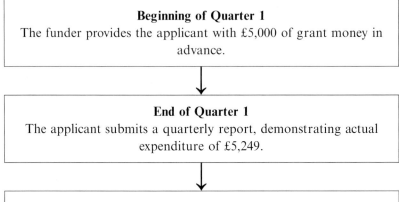

Beginning of Quarter 1
The funder provides the applicant with £5,000 of grant money in advance.

End of Quarter 1
The applicant submits a quarterly report, demonstrating actual expenditure of £5,249.

Beginning of Quarter 2
The funder provides the applicant with £5,249 of grant money, comprising £249 to cover the extra expenditure actually incurred in Quarter 1, and the next £5,000 in advance for Quarter 2.

End of Quarter 2
The applicant submits a quarterly report, demonstrating £4,589 worth of expenditure for this period.

Beginning of Quarter 3
The funder provides the applicant with £4,589 of grant money. Add this to the £411 of grant money not used from the last quarter's advance (£5,000 minus £4,589). This means that the applicant has still received £5,000 of grant money in advance.

...and so it goes on.

Not all funders are happy, or able to do this, but unless you ask, you won't find out! A funder might notice during the appraisal process that the project may be too big for the community group to tackle. This is when a funder may question whether you are the right group to run the project. If you're going to run into financial difficulties, then the project may not develop as well as you anticipate. If your project is the right project to solve the problems that you've identified, be prepared to accept that another community group, such as the parish council, may be better placed financially to deliver the project.

PROVIDING EVIDENCE OF YOUR CLAIM

Cynical lot these funding organisations aren't they? Not only do you have to prove to them that you need the grant money in the first place, but you also have to demonstrate exactly what you've spent their money on by keeping hold of all the receipts and invoices! Next, they'll be asking for your blood!

Well, before you throw your hands up in despair, let's just take a step back for a minute and look at the wider picture. Don't forget that it isn't your money that you are spending – it's theirs. They have a right to know how much of their money you have spent, what you've spent it on and whether you have actually spent it as you said you would on your application form. And if your funding organisation is a local authority, or an organisation who obtain their funding from either the national government, or Europe, then it's tax payers' money they are giving to you. They have a responsibility to account for that money, and may be liable to inspections from either the National Audit Office or European auditors.

If you've ever had to complete your own personal tax return for those other lovely people at Her Majesty's Revenue and Customs, then you'll know how important paper records are. Create a file where all of your invoices and receipts can be kept together. This will make completing the claim form much easier in the future. You can't change the funding organisation's rules for claiming, but you can ensure that your claim is correct. Correct claims are processed speedily, and maximise the amount of grant available to you. So what sort of evidence do you have to provide?

Invoices

Invoices are the first step in demonstrating that goods and services have been supplied. However, each invoice needs to contain specific information for a funder to check that it is genuine and relates to your project.

- **Headed paper**. The invoice should clearly display the supplier's name, address and a logo (if they have one). If a company doesn't do this, might it have something to hide? Would you feel comfortable buying something personally from an organisation that you couldn't contact afterwards?

- **Addressed to you**. The invoice should be addressed to your community group. If it's not addressed to the group then it isn't *your* invoice. Would you pay the electricity bill for your next-door neighbour? However, it is quite common for invoices to be addressed and sent to the person from the community group who ordered the equipment or services in the first place. Many suppliers will be happy to amend the 'Invoice to' details and issue a replacement, but this takes time. If you only spot it when it's time to make a claim, this error will delay your claim and possibly your grant payment. Get it right in the first place, by giving clear instructions to those in your community group who will be spending the money. Invoices must be addressed to the community group (not the person ordering the goods or services), although a 'care of' address (such as the Treasurer's address) can be used.

- **In date**. For the invoice to be valid, it needs to be dated after the date of the offer letter from your funder. If your project has received a 'Permission to Start' notice, only invoices dated after this will be valid. If the invoice is dated before, it suggests that work began on your project before you'd received your offer letter. Funders will classify these invoices as ineligible and you cannot make a claim against them.

- **VAT registered**. If the supplier is VAT registered, the VAT registration number should be clearly visible on the invoice. Only if the supplier is VAT registered should they be charging VAT on the invoice. The VAT registration number is important because there are some organisations that can claim back the VAT on purchases, such as parish councils. If a project can reclaim the VAT, then grant money isn't needed to cover this cost. VAT invoices should also make it clear, which of the supplied items have VAT charged on them, and at what rate. VAT invoices should contain the following information:

  1. Supplier's name, address and VAT registration number.

  2. A unique identifying number to distinguish it from other invoices from the same supplier.

  3. The date of issue of the invoice, and also the date the goods or services were provided, if this is different to the date of the invoice.

  4. Your community group's name and address – who the goods or services were supplied to.

  5. The type of the supply – were the goods sold or hired to you?

  6. A description of the goods or services supplied (which should break down the information further by detailing the quantity of goods or services supplied, the cost before VAT, the rate of VAT applicable for those goods or services, the total charge excluding VAT, and the total VAT charge).

- **Identify the goods and services supplied**. The invoice needs to clearly state what exactly has been supplied and the cost. Would you pay an invoice if you didn't know what it was for? Funding organisations will check the items on an invoice to ensure that they are required for the project. If your project is to refurbish the community centre, the funder will question an invoice for two nights' accommodation at a hotel fifty miles away! This example may be extreme, but if your project is funded by several organisations, who will only support specific expenditure, it's important that they see the right invoices. An organisation only willing to support the sporting element of your community centre refurbishment may be happy to pay for building works relating to the creation of a shower block and changing facilities, but they won't want to pay for the small computer suite that you're also creating. Correct narration on invoices helps funders to clarify which invoices they can release grant monies against.

- **Paid**. Some funders may only release grant monies against paid invoices. This is called 'defrayed expenditure'. Until an invoice has been paid, it can be cancelled, or a partial credit can be applied for the return of some of the goods. If a funder releases money against an invoice that hasn't been paid, the opportunity for fraud increases. (An applicant could submit an invoice, claim the grant money and then return the goods to the supplier for a refund, keeping the grant money.) Having the word 'PAID' stamped onto an invoice doesn't prove it's been paid either – nor does it prove that the community group themselves paid it. All it proves is that the word 'PAID' has been stamped on the invoice! To prove payment, the funder may want to see evidence of your bank account statements. We'll look at this in more detail later on in this chapter.

- **Be an invoice**. Yes, an invoice needs to declare that it is an invoice. Funders won't release grant monies against delivery notes, for example. Goods and services don't have to be paid for by the same people that actually receive them. If your employer buys some reference books for you, the invoice may go to head office, but the books and delivery note will go direct to you. Proof of delivery does not mean proof of payment. Invoices should also have a unique reference number to help distinguish it from other invoices from the same supplier.

Receipts

Apart from invoices, the other evidence of expenditure that you may come across are cash receipts. It's quite possible for a relatively small project to have nothing but cash receipts. These are still vital to your claim though. Funders will want to see them. Most shops provide quite detailed receipts, which include:

- retailer's name;
- date of purchase;
- description of item;
- amount;
- total figure.

VAT registered groups should get into the habit of asking for VAT receipts from retailers, which will include additional information such as a VAT registration number.

It is possible that you could have difficulty with till-roll receipts where only the cost of the product you have purchased is recorded, and not a description. Check with your funding organisation whether they are happy to accept such receipts as evidence. They may be happy to accept them for relatively small amounts, but they might ask for receipts that are more detailed on higher cost items. The problem with a receipt without a description is that it doesn't prove it is related to that project.

Proving payment

A funder may accept a certified statement of income and expenditure, listing all of the money you have received in and paid out for your project along with the original invoices and receipts to back up your figures. Certification means that the Treasurer or the group's accountant has signed the statement to say that the information is true and accurate. If you're unsure what is needed, speak with your funder.

Some funders may ask you to supply copies of your bank statements. Only when your bank account has been debited for the amount in question has the invoice actually been paid. It therefore helps you, and the funders, if you clearly link the invoice to the cheque stub.

When you pay an invoice by cheque, write the date that you paid (or posted) the cheque and the cheque number on the relevant invoice. This links the two together nicely, and the funder will be able to pick up from your bank statements the date that the cheque number was debited to your account. If the supplier subsequently issues you with a statement of account, or receipt acknowledging your payment, keep this together with the actual invoice.

Petty cash

You should have a system in place to deal with petty cash claims from community group members for small items of expenditure. If you need a book of raffle tickets, it's unreasonable to ask the newsagent to supply an invoice. Let someone pay for them and, as long as they obtain a receipt, you can reimburse them. Make a record of what was purchased, who purchased the item, and the date that they were reimbursed. Ideally, the person receiving the money should sign to say that have received it, to avoid any disputes in the future.

Using records to make a claim

In Chapter 8 it was suggested that you should keep a list of all the invoices and receipts received for your project, number them in numerical order, and identify which expenditure category they fall into. When the time comes to make a claim, this makes life so much easier. Let's imagine your list of invoices and receipts for your project to hold a street party looks as follows:

Table 21. List of project expenditure

Ref. no	Amount	Supplier	Description	Expenditure category	Date paid	Chq no
001	£150.00	Parties R Us	Trestle table hire	Equipment	01/08/XX	100239
002	£80.00	Mr Funny the Clown	Children's entertainer	Entertainment	26/08/XX	100250
003	£83.46	Local supermarket	Food supplies	Food	19/08/XX	100245
004	£50.00	Art Face	Face painter	Entertainment	26/08/XX	100249
005	£65.00	DJ Slimbloke	Music entertainment	Entertainment	26/08/XX	100244
006	£37.62	Parties R Us	Plastic plates, cups and cutlery	Equipment	07/08/XX	100242
007	£61.06	Local supermarket	Drinks and refreshments	Food	22/08/XX	100248
008	£43.85	Parties R Us	Balloons and streamers	Equipment	17/08/XX	100243
009	£150.00	Local supermarket	Raffle prizes	Equipment	21/08/XX	100247
010	£1.50	Stationers	Raffle tickets	Stationery	18/08/XX	Petty cash
011	£75.00	Local council	Road closure	Fees	20/08/XX	100246
012	£50	Local council	Entertainment licence	Fees	02/08/XX	100241
013	£12.99	Stationers	Leaflets/ invitations	Stationery	01/08/XX	100240

Although monitoring forms vary from funder to funder, there may not be the room on them to list every item of expenditure, so you'll be asked to give summary totals for each set of expenditure category. It's best if you use the same expenditure categories that you used on your original application form. If you've maintained a list like that in the example, as you go about your project, then providing the information in summary form is very easy. If you use a spreadsheet on a computer, the spreadsheet can even do this for you.

So, revise your list, sorting all the information in expense categories, as follows:

Table 22 – Equipment summary

Ref. no	Amount	Supplier	Description	Expenditure category	Date paid	Chq no
001	£150.00	Parties R Us	Trestle table hire	Equipment	01/08/XX	100239
006	£37.62	Parties R Us	Plastic plates, cups and cutlery	Equipment	07/08/XX	100242
008	£43.85	Parties R Us	Balloons and streamers	Equipment	17/08/XX	100243
009	£150.00	Local supermarket	Raffle prizes	Equipment	21/08/XX	100247
	£381.47	**Total expenditure on equipment**				

The table above shows all the expenditure that relates to equipment for the project, and tells us that we need invoices 001, 006, 008 and 009 to use as our documentary evidence. The following tables show the breakdown for each of the other categories, gives a total figure for each category to transfer onto our monitoring form, and it also demonstrates which invoices and receipts are required.

Table 23. Entertainment summary

Ref no	Amount	Supplier	Description	Expenditure category	Date paid	Chq no
002	£80.00	Mr Funny the Clown	Children's entertainer	Entertainment	26/08/XX	100250
004	£50.00	Art Face	Face painter	Entertainment	26/08/XX	100249
005	£65.00	DJ Slimboke	Music entertainment	Entertainment	26/08/XX	100244
	£195.00	Total expenditure on entertainment				

Table 24. Food summary

Ref. no	Amount	Supplier	Description	Expenditure category	Date paid	Chq no
003	£83.46	Local supermarket	Food supplies	Food	19/08/XX	100245
007	£61.06	Local supermarket	Drinks and refreshments	Food	22/08/XX	100248
	£144.52	**Total expenditure on food**				

Table 25. Stationery summary

Ref. no	Amount	Supplier	Description	Expenditure category	Date paid	Chq no
010	£1.50	Stationers	Raffle tickets	Stationery	18/08/XX	Petty cash
013	£12.99	Stationers	Leaflets/ invitations	Stationery	01/08/XX	100240
	£14.49	**Total expenditure on stationery**				

Table 26. Fees summary

Ref. no	Amount	Supplier	Description	Expenditure category	Date paid	Chq no
011	£75.00	Local council	Road closure	Fees	20/08/XX	100246
012	£50.00	Local council	Entertainment licence	Fees	02/08/XX	100241
	£125.00	**Total expenditure on fees**				

Whilst the only figures you need to put on your monitoring form will probably be the total expenditure figures for each category, it is sensible to include a copy of this breakdown with your claim. Not only does it give you a checklist to make sure that you have all of the invoices you need to send off with your claim, but it also gives your funder a checklist to ensure that nothing is missing. This extra information demonstrates how you have arrived at the figures that you have entered onto your claim form.

PROVIDING EVIDENCE OF IN-KIND SUPPORT

We saw earlier how it's possible to put a monetary value on the volunteer time provided by local people and other members of the community group. This in-kind support contribution will need to appear on your monitoring form as a cost but also as a form of income. Once again though, we need to demonstrate to the funders how we arrived at the summary figure.

If volunteer time will form part of your project, always obtain an hourly rate from your funder, and get it in writing. When it's time to complete your monitoring form, gather together all of the signed, completed volunteer timesheets.

Table 27. Completed volunteer sheet

B. G. G. C. Volunteer Name: Fred Carrott Volunteer's Address: Carrott Lodge, Sprout Lane, Bevel Gate		Bevel Gate Community Garden Project		
Date	Description of activities	Start time	End time	No. of hours
17/01/XX	Clearing of community garden area	13.00	16.00	3
18/01/XX	Erection of boundary fences	13.00	17.30	4.5
19/01/XX	Spreading topsoil	09.00	10.30	1.5
		Total hours volunteered		9.00
Volunteer signature: *Fred Carrott*				

If there are several volunteers, you might find it useful to create a summary sheet transferring all the names and the total number of hours volunteered.

Table 28. Summary volunteer sheet

Volunteer name	Total number of hours volunteered
Fred Carrott	9.00
George Potato	1.5
Elizabeth Bean	8.5
Cathy Leek	5.5
Chris Berry	7.25
Total hours volunteered =	**31.75**

Let's imagine that your funder has advised you that the hourly rate you can apply to volunteer time is £9 per hour. The total monetary value for all of those volunteers' help is:

31.75 hours × by £9 per hour = £285.75

You would include the £285.75 in the expenditure section of your monitoring report, because it represents a cost of work carried out. However, because it is in-kind support, you are not being charged for it (the volunteers gave up their time for the project), so you should include the total figure of £285.75 in the income section as well. This often seems confusing to some people because if you include the figure in both the income and the expenditure sections, then they cancel each other out – which they should do because it isn't money that you've physically had to pay out. However, you may recall from Chapter 4 that this in-kind support can help you increase your percentage of the contribution towards your project. As this affects your contribution, it also impacts upon the intervention rates of the other funders in your project, which is why you must record it in your monitoring form and statement of income and expenditure.

Other in-kind support

In-kind support can also be provided by suppliers who are willing to provide goods or services without charge. Perhaps they are happy to hire you some tools for the day free of charge, or give you some equipment for free. While the temptation may be to shake their hands and run away quickly before they change their minds, you need to think about your monitoring forms! Once again, you're going to need to prove the cost of the contribution to your funders. The easiest way to do this is to ask the supplier to issue you with an invoice which clearly demonstrates the cost of the goods or services but has the phrase 'In-kind support – please do not pay this invoice' printed on it. This proves to anyone looking through your claim that the cost you've put down on your monitoring form is correct, and not just a number you've made up, whilst the phrase clearly identifies that it is in-kind support.

The Bevelshire Partnership

Bevel Gate Tool Hire

High Street

Bevel Gate

17/01/XX

Bevel Gate Gardening Club

c/o The Treasurer

Clive Cucumber

The Greenhouses

Garden Crescent

Bevel Gate

INVOICE

Inv. No. 1874

Date of Supply 17/01/XX

Description	Amount
Hire of rotavator for half day	£45.00
Subtotal	£45.00
VAT at 17.5%	£7.87
Total	**£52.87**

IN-KIND SUPPORT – PLEASE DO NOT PAY THIS INVOICE

VAT Reg. No. 397 6428 28

Fig. 6. Example of in-kind invoice.

If the invoice does not make it clear that this is in-kind support, the funders may consider that this is an outstanding invoice, still waiting to be paid, and discount it from you claim. If your funder only releases grant money against paid invoices, this will impact on the actual grant payment they make, which could affect your cash flow.

Remember, the rules for invoices still apply to in-kind support invoices. They must clearly state a VAT registration number if the supplier is VAT registered, provide a description of the goods, a breakdown of price and VAT, etc., just like any other invoice.

OVERPAID GRANT MONIES

If your funder releases grant payments upon receipt of paid invoices only then, in theory, an overpayment won't occur. This is because they can see what your actual costs are, and release grant money to you at the agreed intervention rate as per your offer letter, until they reach the total grant figure. However, some funders may release the total amount of grant money upfront. If your project ends up spending less than you anticipated, you will have some grant money remaining.

The income and expenditure sections of your monitoring form should illustrate exactly how much grant money you have left. Ask your funders how they would like you to deal with this. Some may ask you to repay it immediately. If you've received all of your grant money upfront and covered all of your costs, the remaining grant balance should be sitting in your bank account, so you can easily write them out a cheque.

However, before you submit your final monitoring form, stop and have a think for a moment. Is there anything that you could use this remaining money for which relates to your project? This isn't an excuse to nip down the pub and celebrate! If you can identify another useful purchase, don't go and spend the money, but check with your funder first.

For example, if your project was to create a cricket pitch for the local sports club and you underspent by £500, could you use that money to buy something to help maintain the cricket pitch? What about a cover to protect it from the rain? Is there a special attachment that you can buy that fixes onto the grounds maintenance lawnmower to enable you to cut the grass at the right height? If you can identify ways to spend the money to enhance your project further, approach your funder in writing and explain the situation. Many funders will be willing to allow you to go ahead, but only if you've asked first!

> ## NEVER SHOP FIRST AND THEN ASK AFTERWARDS

Not only is it rude, it might be a breach of the original grant conditions, and you don't want to jeopardise the entire project just to spend the remaining few pounds of grant money.

But what happens if there's been a mistake and a funder has overpaid you? This doesn't happen very often, and intervention rates are used to help reduce this risk. However, if you identify that you've been overpaid, contact your funder immediately. Communication is the key to resolving this. Remain calm and courteous at all times.

If it is the funder's error, and the amount is relatively small, they may allow you to keep the overpayment. This may also depend upon where the funder's money comes from. If it is from the public purse, the funding organisation is more likely to want it returned. However, they may also consider the practicality of re-obtaining the funds. Ending up in a court of law is costly and not good publicity for either party.

It's also possible that if your project involves two or three phases, any overpayment can be carried forward into the next phase. If this happens, the offer letter for the new phase will reflect this accordingly.

BEVEL GATE GARDENING CLUB'S CLAIM

Bevel Gate Gardening Club has completed its monitoring form, which will enable it to claim the outstanding grant money. The statement of income and expenditure shows that the total project costs were slightly higher than anticipated at £9,119.07. The offer letter from the Bevelshire Partnership said that their grant was for £6,150 or 67.95 per cent, whichever was the lesser. Using the intervention rate of 67.95 per cent to calculate the grant figure, based upon the group's total project costs, gives a total of £6,196.41.

$$£9,119.07 \times 67.95\% = £6,196.41$$

However, because of the phrase 'whichever is the lesser', the funder will only release £6,150, because this is less than £6,196.41. The total project costs are £69.07 higher than expected (£9,119.07 minus £9,050.00), so Bevel Gate Gardening Club has had to find this extra money from its own resources.

The Bevelshire Partnership

The Bevelshire Partnership, Bevelshire House, Beveltown, Bevelshire BV1 1TN

ENVIRONMENTAL GRANT SCHEME
END-OF-PROJECT MONITORING FORM

To enable us to assess the impact of your project and the value of our funding, please complete and return this form within the next 30 days, and include any photographic evidence, invoices and paperwork to substantiate your statements. Please note that failure to complete this form properly or withholding evidence will result in a delay in your final grant payment being released. As per our offer letter, your project may be audited by an external auditor to ensure probity, and 5% of your grant monies may be withheld until this process is complete.

PROJECT CONTACT DETAILS

Project name: Bevel Gate Community Garden Project

Project reference: HL/BGComGar

Grant offered: £6,150 or 67.95%

Community group: Bevel Gate Gardening Club

Contact name: Mr R. Weed

Contact address: Bevel Gate Gardening Club, c/o The Grass Cuttings, Bevel Gate, Bevelshire, BV12 1VB

Contact telephone number: 01657 943048

Contact email: rweed@bggardeningclub.co.uk

PROJECT DETAILS

Please provide a brief description of what your project wanted to achieve:

Fig. 7. Bevel Gate Gardening Club end-of-project monitoring form.

The Bevel Gate Community Garden Project wanted to clear and level the 1,750 square metre site of wasteland that we own (through a generous gift from one of our members) adjacent to the Community Centre. To begin with, the land was overgrown with weeds and had several large earth banks. Once the land had been cleared of weeds and levelled, we wanted to remove the topsoil to a depth of three feet and replace it with new topsoil. Water and electricity supplies would then be installed. The site, which is 25 metres wide by 70 metres long, was then to be split into two, to create a practical facility where club members and community residents could learn gardening techniques. The second area would be turned into a wildlife garden where residents could sit and relax. The fresh produce grown on the community garden will be sold to the local community.

When did your project start: 2 January 20YY

When did you complete your project: 27 February 20YY is when the project was physically completed.

MILESTONES

Did you meet your milestones as planned?

Milestone	Target	Achieved?
1st weekend in January 20YY	Volunteers clear excess undergrowth.	Yes.
2nd weekend in January 20YY	Site cleared using hire equipment, old topsoil removed.	Yes.
3rd week in January	Electricity and water companies install services.	Yes – electricity was installed at the beginning of the week, and the water at the end of the week.
3rd weekend in January 20YY	Replacement topsoil delivered. Volunteers begin creating community garden infrastructure – raised beds, wildlife pond and pathways. Boundary fence erected around community garden perimeter.	Top soil delivered on time. Infrastructure begun on time, during third week. Fencing couldn't be erected until last week in January.

4th weekend in January 20YY	Gardening Club storage shed erected.	Yes – shed erected at same time as boundary fencing.
3rd weekend in February 20YY	Communal garden equipment purchased.	Yes, most was purchased at the beginning of February.
4^h weekend in February 20YY	Wildlife garden planting completed.	All plants that could be planted at this time of year were planted.

PROJECT IMPLEMENTATION

Please provide a description of how your project proceeded:

Our project began on the first weekend in January when 26 volunteers helped to clear the excess undergrowth from the site. Despite the cold weather, the exercise helped to keep us warm! On the second weekend, the rotavator and earth-moving equipment enabled us to clear the topsoil and remaining undergrowth in one day, which was better than anticipated. With the ground prepared, utility companies came in and installed two electrical and water points within the community garden. The new topsoil was delivered the following weekend, and volunteers then began creating the practical gardening area, and started the hard landscaping for the wildlife garden. Unfortunately, the fencing company couldn't erect the new boundary fence until the following weekend, when the shed was constructed. In the meantime, members from the project committee acquired the plants, seeds, general tools and equipment we were looking for, and by the final weekend in February, the volunteers gave a final push and completed the wildlife garden. Now, Mother Nature needs to do her bit!

Were there any aspects of the project that didn't go well?

We had problems with the fencing company erecting the boundary fence. Staffing problems meant that they couldn't do this as planned on 19 January 20YY as booked, but they were able to carry out this work the following weekend (25 January 20YY).

Did anything work well?

We felt that the organisation of the volunteers worked well. One of the project committee members created a tick sheet, which was given to every volunteer, making it clear what they needed to do to enable us to include their efforts in our claim. As a result, we had very few problems with volunteer timesheets. Although several of the volunteers felt that the timesheets were 'very bureaucratic', they understood why we were using them, and their importance to us.

PROJECT OUTPUTS

Did you achieve the outputs you set out to achieve?

Output	Target	Achieved?
Number of new community facilities created	2	Yes – the Gardening Club members have plenty of plans for the coming months for getting their hands dirty, and we've received positive feedback from the community concerning the wildlife garden (see photos enclosed).
Number of additional people using new community facility	629	391 people visited the wildlife garden when we opened it to the public, and more are expected to visit over the summer months.
Number of volunteers directly involved with the project	25	26 people helped out (see volunteer sheets).
Number of people given access to new learning opportunities.	190	198 people from the club and local residents have put their names down for days when we shall be running practical activities in the garden.
Area of land enhanced	1750sqm	1750 square metres of land have been improved (see photos enclosed).

PROJECT OUTCOMES

Please list the outcomes of your project and whether any have been achieved. What action will you take to measure these outcomes?

1. Increased knowledge and skills in gardening and wildlife management.

▶

2. Improved community spirit – community garden will give residents a new shared, common interest with each other.

3. Increased awareness of seasonality of produce through the sale of our own community garden produce.

4. Increased awareness of local wildlife and environmental issues.

5. It is too early at this stage to say whether these outcomes have been achieved, although the 26 volunteers who helped to clear the land have already made anecdotal comments about feeling part of the community. We intend to undertake a survey at the end of 20YY to collect this information.

PROJECT FINANCES

Please complete the statement of income and expenditure section overleaf, and provide all evidence of expenditure (receipts, bank statements, cheque books) along with this claim. Please note that the Bevelshire Partnership may ask an external auditor to examine your claim and documentary evidence.

STATEMENT OF INCOME AND EXPENDITURE
Expenditure

Expenditure item	Expenditure category	Projected cost	Actual cost
Hire of rotavator, skip and earth mover for two days (in-kind)	Equipment hire	£500.00	£500.00
Topsoil removal and disposal. Replacement topsoil	Land improvements	£2,300.00	£2,364.56
Installation of electricity and water	Utilities	£2,500.00	£2,500.00
Seats, benches and paving	Equipment	£500.00	£495.62
Plants and seed	Equipment	£500.00	£504.38
Shed, communal garden equipment	Equipment	£650.00	£652.89
Boundary fence and gate	Security fixtures	£1,200.00	£1,201.62
Volunteer time (in-kind)	Volunteer	£900.00	£900.00
Totals		**£9,050.00**	**£9,119.07**

Income

Funding	Projected	Actual
In-kind equipment hire	£500.00	£500.00
In-kind volunteer time	£900.00	£900.00
First 75% of grant from Bevelshire Partnership Healthy Living Grant Scheme	£4,612.50	£4,612.50
Applicant contribution (Bevel Gate Gardening Club)	£1,500.00	£1,569.07
Outstanding grant payment due	£1,537.50	£1,537.50
Totals	**£9,050.00**	**£9,119.07**

I certify that this statement of income and expenditure is true and accurate, and I enclose copies of all our financial records as evidence.

Signed *B. Beanpole* (Position in Group) *Treasurer*

DECLARATION

I certify that the information in this end-of-project monitoring form is an accurate reflection of the project and what it has achieved.

Signed *R. Weed* Date 22/03/20YY (Position in Group) *Chairman*

10
Project Completion

Hooray! It's been a long journey but your project is now complete. Congratulations! It's all paid for and the local community are enjoying the benefits. You can put your feet up, relax, have a party, break open a bottle of champagne, or put the kettle on to celebrate. Let's face it – you deserve it. It's all over now, and you can go back to your ordinary, pre-project boring life. Can't you? Actually, this might not be the end. In the same way that it was necessary to collect some baseline information at the start of your application process, it may be necessary to collect some further information to show what impact your project has had.

EVALUATION

It's understandable that some funders want to find out whether their money has actually made a difference. There may also be some outputs that you can't count once your project is complete. For example, if your tourist leaflet is printed and distributed for the beginning of the tourist season, you won't know what effect it has had until the end of the season. That doesn't mean that you escape the need to have to find out! Your funders may make a note and contact you in the future, asking you to report to them regarding this particular output. This means that your final claim form might not be the final monitoring form that you complete. The project evaluation is effectively the final monitoring form, and it may look similar to other monitoring forms that you've completed. The final monitoring or evaluation form will want to:

- Examine whether the project achieved what it set out to achieve.

- Identify any difficulties that were encountered and how they were resolved.
- Whether the project generated any additional benefits.
- What the outcomes were.
- Whether anything could have been done better.

Funders may also use the opportunity to ask questions about how you felt the grant application, claiming and monitoring processes that you had to go through worked. Good funders will always seek feedback on how they can improve their systems.

Whilst many project outputs can be counted and achieved by the time the project is finished, measuring the outcomes of a project can only take place long after this date. For some outcomes, it's a question of measuring people's perceptions. Do they feel that community spirit is much stronger as a result of your project? Do they feel that crime levels have fallen? You might be able to use national government statistics to prove that the actual crime rate has fallen, and if there are national or local authority statistics that are published on a regular basis that you can use, it might be useful to draw upon them. However, those statistics might not reveal the true impact of just your project. Other external factors over which you had no control could influence those figures and distort the true results of your work.

Another survey may be the best solution, because this can indicate people's perceptions. It may be necessary to survey those people you originally surveyed at the beginning, when you were assessing the level of demand for your project. Are there any questions you used on that initial survey which you can use again? Comparing the results of exactly the same questions on the first and last surveys can highlight the real achievement of your project.

If you're unsure of the best way to evaluate the success of your project, discuss this with your funder, or your contact at the local authority or voluntary support group. And as with all your other forms, always return this final evaluation form by the deadline set, enclosing any additional evidence that illustrates your figures and claims. If this deadline will be difficult to meet for practical reasons, speak to your funder and explain why. Some funders are more flexible than others.

PUBLICITY – FOR YOU AND YOUR FUNDER

Completing a project is something to be proud of, so have a party, or a celebration, and invite all of your funders. Give them another excuse to get out of the office and an opportunity to see what their money has helped you to achieve. Issue press releases, and invite the local paper along. Despite what you may read, they do like good news stories!

Your offer letter and grant guidance notes will identify what your publicity responsibilities are. Although your project is complete, you still have to adhere to the conditions laid down by your funder. Publicity opportunities where funders may expect their support to be acknowledged include:

- your accounts and annual report if you are a charitable organisation;
- job or other advertisements placed in newspapers;
- press releases, or pieces on the local radio;
- information leaflets, or any other written communication with the public;
- physical plaques or stickers on new or refurbished buildings, entrances to new facilities or vehicles bought;
- on the main homepage of a website that has been created.

Contact your funder when you need to use their logo and explain where you will be using it. They will provide you with digital versions to use in documents, websites, press releases and other printed material, and physical versions for plaques and information boards. You will also be advised on any particular wording that you should use such as: 'Supported by the Bevelshire Partnership' or 'Bevel Gate Gardening Club gratefully acknowledge the financial support of the Bevelshire Partnership'.

Funding organisations also have their own publicity machine, generating press releases and keeping their own websites up to date. Whenever a new batch of projects have been awarded financial support, funders often issue press releases to both the national and local press. Be aware that many like to use projects they've supported as 'case studies' or examples to future prospective applicants. Look at the websites of some of the larger funding organisations and you'll see a selection of these case studies that they've supported recently.

Whilst funders are keen to publicise the good news, they will respect a project's wishes to refrain from certain publicity aspects if there is a justifiable reason. This often means projects where confidential advice and support is provided. If you are unsure whether publicity is appropriate, discuss your concerns with your funders. There will always be a solution.

HOW LONG TO KEEP THE PAPERWORK

If you're reading this book from cover to cover to gain an understanding of the whole grant system, you'll probably have gathered by now that despite this being the twenty-first century, there can be a lot of paperwork relating to your project. The temptation to throw it away when everything is completed will probably be quite high. Don't! There may be an auditor lurking somewhere in the future. They may need to come and inspect all of your paperwork, years after your project finished. So how long should you keep your paperwork?

This will depend upon where your funders obtain their money. Anything with a European connection seems to lengthen the timescale dramatically. The number of years may not refer to the timescale after your project finished, but the time when a grant scheme has finished.

Imagine that your project was funded by a new grant scheme run by your local authority. They have successfully won a slice of European money, which will enable them to run a grant scheme for five years. You apply for funding in the first year of the scheme, are successful, and finish your project within that same year. The European funders may instruct your local authority that all paperwork relating to projects should be retained for up to seven years after the end of the grant scheme. Note the phrase 'after the end of the grant scheme'. That doesn't mean that you can dispose of your project paperwork in Year eight, because that would be seven years after *project* completion. Year eight is only the third year after the end of the five year grant scheme, so if paperwork has to be kept for seven years after the scheme finished in Year five, it actually means that those projects funded and completed in the first year can only destroy their paperwork in Year thirteen!

Table 29. Document retention

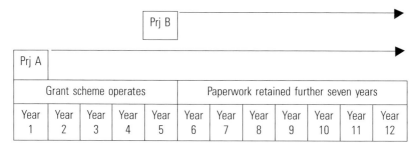

Grant scheme operates					Paperwork retained further seven years						
Year 1	Year 2	Year 3	Year 4	Year 5	Year 6	Year 7	Year 8	Year 9	Year 10	Year 11	Year 12

In the example above, Project A receives a grant and completes its project in Year one. Because the European conditions of grant stipulate that paperwork has to be kept for seven years after the grant scheme has completed, Project A has to keep its paperwork for the remaining four years of the grant scheme, as well as the next seven years. Project B, on the other hand, applies and receives its grant in the final year of the grant scheme, Year five. This project only has to keep the paperwork for the additional seven years.

Check the grant scheme guidelines for advice on how long your paperwork should be kept for, and if it isn't clear, refer to your funder. The European example here is at the more extreme end of retention periods, but you should be aware that you will have to keep hold of the paperwork for some time, and this condition of your grant is just as important as any other.

Keep project records separate

Once your project is complete, keep all the paperwork together in a box designed for paper storage, which you can obtain from many stationers. Write clearly on all sides of the box details of the contents inside and a clear date as to when it can be destroyed. The aim is to make this clear to anyone within the community group, not just those involved with the project. You don't want someone to inadvertently throw the box out whilst having a clear out, and you shouldn't assume that you will be there in the future to destroy it when the time comes.

AND FINALLY

At the beginning of this book, I recommended that you read through the first ten chapters before even beginning to look for funders, just to get a general overview of how grant schemes can operate here in the UK. Now you understand the basics of what might be expected, you may have a little voice at the back of your mind questioning whether it is worth all the effort. Well, tell that little voice to shut up! The answer is a resounding 'yes' – it is worth it. Anything new is always a challenge, but the rewards of applying for grant funding far outweigh any of the drawbacks. The benefits often reach further than the aims of your original project. Having this extra common goal strengthens community groups. Implementing a project may be a challenge, but it's one that you as a group can overcome. The work that you carry out will raise your group's profile within your local community, whether it be in a village, town suburb or city centre estate. This can help to improve the sense of community within that area.

Applying for funding, winning it and then implementing a project, shows determination, an understanding and ability to follow processes, and demonstrates skill at overcoming problems. This is all useful information to include on your CV when approaching employers for a job. (If you can sell your project to a funding organisation, you should be able to sell your skills to a potential employer!)

Once you've successfully completed one project, don't stop there. Where's the next challenge for your group? When a funder receives another application for funding from you, they now have your track record to look back on. They know that you have experience of delivering a project that you set out to achieve, and that you can provide all of the paperwork that is expected of you. Who knows, the project that inspired you to buy this book may turn out to be the first of many. I do hope so – and so do the funders. They want you to achieve your goals just as much as you do. So what are you waiting for? Get to it!

Appendix 1
Glossary

Additionality The 'extra' benefits that grant funding enables a project to provide.

Baseline The starting point or snapshot as things are, before a project begins to make its changes. This information or data is compared with similar data once a project has finished to measure the difference that a project has made.

Beneficiaries The people or groups of people a project is trying to help.

Business plan A list of aims and actions required to achieve them. Might also be used to demonstrate to funders how a project will continue once grant funding has ceased.

Capital expenditure Money spent on physical items, such as buildings or equipment.

Contingency An allowance to cover the unexpected. Some projects, particularly those involving building work, allocate a small sum of money for any unexpected problems that arise.

Criteria The rules funding organisations use to determine which projects or voluntary groups they are keen to support.

Defrayed Costs that have been paid. The invoice has been received and paid and payment has been taken from the bank account.

Eligible Meet the conditions set by a funding organisation.

Evaluation A review at the end of the project to see how successful it has been (what has been achieved), and what could have been done differently or more efficiently.

Forward strategy Details and plans about what will happen in the future. Some funders ask for a forward strategy for projects establishing new facilities or services, so they know how they will continue to operate once grant funding has finished.

In-kind contributions A contribution given to a project, which has a monetary value, but no charge is made. This could include volunteers offering their time, or businesses who lend or give equipment that they would normally charge for.

Match funding Where more than one funding organisation provides a grant to the same project. The grant amounts do not need to match exactly (i.e. be the same amount).

Milestones Important dates during the delivery of a project by which key tasks need to have been achieved.

Monitoring Reviewing what has been achieved so far to see how a project is progressing by gathering information. Some information may need to be collected continuously throughout a project, whilst other data might only be collected at the end.

Option appraisal Identifying the different options or opportunities that may be used to solve the problem, and then analysing them to see which is the best solution.

Outcome The impact a project has on a community. Measuring the impact may only be possible after a period of time.

Output A specific, measurable result produced by the project.

Revenue expenditure Day-to-day running costs such as electricity, rent, telephone bills and other overheads.

Sustainability The ability for a project to continue running in the future without further support from the funding organisation, particularly if there will still be demand for the project.

Value for money An assessment of whether the grant funding requested is an efficient use of money to achieve the outputs or outcomes.

Appendix 2
Funding Organisations and Trusts

Here are a few of the thousands of funding organisations that exist in the UK. Always ask for a copy of their latest eligibility criteria before completing an application form.

ARTS

Arts Council England, 14 Great Peter Street, London SW1P 3NQ. www.artscouncil.org.uk/funding/index.php. Arts Council England is subdivided into several regions. Visit www.artscouncil.org.uk/regions/index.php to find the contact details of your region.

Arts Council of Northern Ireland, 77 Malone Road, Belfast BT9 6AQ. www.artscouncil-ni.org/subpages/funding.htm

Arts Council Wales, www.artswales.org.uk. Arts Council Wales is subdivided into three regions. Visit www.artswales.org/choosearea.asp for further contact details.

Isle of Man Arts Council, St Andrew's House, Finch Road, Douglas IM1 2PX.
www.gov.im/artscouncil/artscommunity.xml

Scottish Arts Council, 12 Manor Place, Edinburgh E3 7DD. www.scottisharts.org.uk/1/funding.aspx

CONSERVATION

Natural England, www.naturalengland.org.uk/conservation/grants-funding/default.htm. Natural England is subdivided into several regions. Visit www.naturalengland.org.uk/contact/default.htm for further contact details.

Scottish Natural Heritage, Great Glen House, Leachkin Road, Inverness IV3 8NW. www.snh.org.uk/about/ab-grants.asp

FOUNDATIONS

The Co-operative Foundation, The Charity Manager, United Co-operatives, Sandbrook Park, Sandbrook Way, Rochdale OL11 1RY. Tel: 01706 202032. www.united.coop/Foundation.asp. Provides grants of between £500 and £30,000 to the community and voluntary sector within the Co-op trading area (see website for details).

Lloyds TSB Foundation for England and Wales, 3rd Floor, 4 St Dunstan's Hill, London EC3R 8UL. www. lloydstsb foundations.org.uk. Offers grants to charities and small community-based charities for projects that will improve people's lives. The Lloyds TSB Foundation has regional offices across England and Wales. Visit www.lloydstsb foundation.org.uk/ourregions.html for contact details.

Lloyds TSB Foundation for the Channel Islands, Lloyds TSB House, 25 New Street, St Helier, Jersey, CI JE4 8RG. Tel: 01534 284201. www.ltsbfoundationci.org/

Lloyds TSB Foundation for Northern Ireland, The Gate Lodge, 73a Malone Road, Belfast BT9 6SB.
www.ltsbfoundationni.org/

Lloyds TSB Foundation for Scotland, Riverside House, 502 Gorgie Road, Edinburgh EH11 3AF.
www.lloydstsbfoundationforscotland.org.uk

Nationwide Foundation, Nationwide House, Pipers Way, Swindon SN38 2SN. www.nationwidefoundation.org.uk. Offers grants to charitable organisations, which meet its current funding criteria (reviewed regularly).

HERITAGE

Most organisations below offer grants to charities and community groups including faith groups, to help preserve historic buildings. See **Heritage Lottery Fund** in lottery-funded schemes below.

Cadw, Welsh Assembly Government, Plas Carew, Unit 5/7 Cefn Coed, Parc Nantgarw, Cardiff CF15 7QQ.
www.cadw.wales.gov.uk

English Heritage, www.english-heritage.org.uk. English Heritage is divided into nine regions. To find the address for your region visit www.english-heritage.org.uk/server/show/CanWebDoc. 4675. Visit www.english-heritage.org.uk/server/show/nav.1120 for more information or email grants@english-heritage.org.uk

Environment and Heritage Service Northern Ireland, 5–33 Hill Street, Belfast BT1 2LA.
www.ehsni.gov.uk/buildings.grants.shtml

Historic Scotland, Salisbury Place, Edinburgh EH9 1SH.
www.historic-scotland.gov.uk/grants

LOTTERY

(Please note that lottery-funded schemes are subject to change.)
www.lotteryfunding.org.uk. Tel: 0845 275 0000.

Awards for All, www.awardsforall.org.uk. Tel: 0845 600 20 40 to be put in contact with your nearest centre. Offers grants for arts, sports, health, education, environment, heritage and community activities.

Big Lottery Fund, www.biglotteryfund.org.uk. Tel: 0845 4 10 20 30 to be put in contact with your nearest centre or for advice on current funding schemes.

Heritage Lottery Fund, www.hlf.org.uk. Tel: 020 7591 6000 to be put in contact with your nearest centre. Offers grants to help people get the most from our historic buildings, natural and cultural heritage.

The following lottery-funded schemes offer grants for sporting projects.

Sport England, 3rd Floor, Victoria House, Bloomsbury Square, London WC1B 4SE. www.sportengland.org Tel: 0845 8 508 508 to be put in contact with your nearest regional centre.

Sportscotland, Caledonia House, South Gyle, Edinburgh EH12 9DQ. www.sportscotland.org.uk

Sports Council for Northern Ireland, House of Sport, Upper Malone Road, Belfast BT9 5LA. www.sportni.net

Sports Council for Wales, Sophia Gardens, Cardiff CF11 9SW. www.sports-council-wales.co.uk

SOCIAL

Comic Relief UK, 5th Floor, 89 Albert Embankment, London SE1 7TP. www.comicrelief.com/applyforagrant/grants-uk.shtml.. Offers grants to charities and community groups with projects that support young or old people, mental health, refugees and asylum seekers, help victims of domestic violence and disadvantaged communities.

Government Funding, www.governmentfunding.org.uk. This useful website allows you to search for grants available from various government departments that are open to the voluntary sector and community groups.

SPORTS

See the other sports schemes listed under the **Lottery** funders.

Football Foundation, 30 Gloucester Place, London W1U 8FF. www.footballfoundation.org.uk/seeking-funding. Various schemes to help communities upgrade stadia, obtain kit and extend social inclusion in the game.

YOUTH

BBC Children In Need, www.bbc.co.uk/pudsey/about_us/grants.shtml. Offers grants to organisations that work and help disadvantaged or young people in the UK.

Help Yourselves, Save The Children, 5th Floor, Hawthorns House, Halfords Lane, Smethwick, West Midlands B66 1BB. www.helpyourselves.org.uk Joint scheme between Save the Children and British Gas to help adults and children work together in community projects.

Appendix 3
Other Helpful Organisations

FUNDING ADVICE AND VOLUNTARY/ COMMUNITY GROUP SUPPORT

Voluntary Action/Council for Voluntary Services

England

National Association for Voluntary and Community Action, 177 Arundel Street, Sheffield S1 2NU. Tel: 0114 278 6636. www.nacva.org.uk

Scotland

Scottish Council for Voluntary Organisations, Mansfield Traquair Centre, 15 Mansfield Place, Edinburgh EH3 6BB. Tel: 0800 169 0022. www.scvo.org.uk

Wales

Welsh Council for Voluntary Action. Six area offices spread across Wales. Tel: 0870 607 1666. www.wcva.org.uk

Northern Ireland

Northern Ireland Community Voluntary Action, 61 Duncairn Gardens, Belfast BT15 2GB. Tel: 028 9087 7777. www.nicva.org/

Rural community councils (England only)

Action with Communities in Rural England, Somerford Court, Somerford Road, Cirencester, Gloucestershire GL7 1TW. www.acre.org.uk/

Other organisations

Community Foundation Network
Arena House, 66–68 Pentonville Road, London N1 9HS.
Tel: 020 7713 9326. www.communityfoundations.org.uk

VolResource
Useful information for any voluntary sector or community group.
www.volresource.org.uk

PARISH COUNCILS

To help locate parish council details in England, visit the National
Association of Local Councils www.nalc.gov.uk/links/index.html
and click on your county for links to further information.

RESEARCH AND INFORMATION

Department for Communities and Local Government, Eland House,
Bressenden Place, London SW1E 5DU. www.statistics.gov.uk

Directory of Social Change, 24 Stephenson Way, London NW1
2DP. www.dsc.org.uk

Neighbourhood Renewal Unit, www.neighbourhood.gov.uk

Social Exclusion Unit, www.socialexclusionunit.gov.uk

Index